D1389439

Sad Topographies

First published in Great Britain by Simon & Schuster UK Ltd, 2017

A CBS COMPANY

1 3 5 7 9 10 8 6 4 2

Simon & Schuster UK Ltd
1st Floor
222 Gray's Inn Road
London WC1X 8HB

www.simonandschuster.co.uk
www.simonandschuster.com.au
www.simonandschuster.co.in

Simon & Schuster Australia, Sydney
Simon & Schuster India, New Delhi

The author and publishers have made all reasonable efforts to contact
copyright-holders for permission, and apologise for any omissions or errors in
the form of credits given. Corrections may be made to future printings.

A CIP catalogue record for this book is available from the British Library

Hardback ISBN: 978-1-4711-6929-8
eBook ISBN: 978-1-4711-6930-4

ART DIRECTION AND DESIGN:
N. Taylor

EDITORIAL:
Caroline Blake and Jo Whitford

ILLUSTRATIONS:
Kateryna Didyk

Sad Topographies
Damien Rudd

Simon & Schuster UK

… a wild dedication of yourselves
To unpath'd waters, undream'd shores; most certain
To miseries enough…

WILLIAM SHAKESPEARE
The Winter's Tale

Sad

adjective \ 'sad \

Feeling or showing sorrow or unhappiness.

Synonyms: blue, brokenhearted, cast down, crestfallen, dejected, depressed, despondent, disconsolate, doleful, down, downcast, downhearted, down in the mouth, droopy, forlorn, gloomy, glum, heartbroken, heartsick, heavyhearted, inconsolable, joyless, low, melancholic, miserable, mournful, saddened, sorrowful, sorry, unhappy, woebegone, woeful, wretched

Introduction

'I hate travelling and explorers.' This is the sentence Claude Lévi-Strauss chose to open his anthropological memoir and travelogue, *Tristes Tropiques* – first published in France in 1955 and translated into English in 1961. Lévi-Strauss dryly declares his disdain for travel books in the opening pages. 'I have often planned to undertake the present work,' he writes, 'but on each occasion a sort of shame and repugnance prevented me making a start.' The book's original French title remains untranslated, as the proposed English translations of 'Sad Tropics' or 'Tropics of Sadness' lacked the subtle poignancy Lévi-Strauss intended.

It was in mid-2015 that I happened upon Mount Hopeless. Not the geological landform, but its name on a map of southern Australia; two microscopic words nestled among a tapestry of topographic contour lines. I was struck by the wonderful absurdity of this small discovery – why, I thought to myself, would there be a mountain called Hopeless in the middle of nowhere? I began typing into Google Maps other depressing synonyms, and from behind the omniscient glow of my computer screen, I unearthed a bygone history of my country: Melancholy Waterhole, Disappointment Bay, Misery Island, Starvation Creek, Suicide Point. All this time I had been residing, in Lévi-Strauss's words, among the '…vestiges of a vanished reality'. After several months I had the beginnings of a collection, a kind of cabinet of depressing cartographical curiosities.

It is on maps that we discover the union of landscape and language. They are not objective representations of the world, but products of a mind; a reflection of the mapmaker's culture and experiences, the time and place in which they were made. Maps are documents, artifacts, guides, authorities and stories.

In 1606, Willem Janszoon and his Dutch crew of the *Duyfken* were on an exploratory mission to map the coast of New Guinea when, completely by accident, they stumbled across the unknown continent of Australia. Thinking it was still New Guinea, they inadvertently became the first Europeans to set foot on this undiscovered land. Janszoon found a place, '...inhabited by savage, cruel, black barbarians who slew some of our sailors,' adding that, 'no information was obtained touching the exact situation of the country and regarding the commodities obtainable and in demand there'. Dismayed by these inscrutable people and their impartiality to trade, Janszoon and his crew abandoned their mission, leaving in their wake a scene of bloody violence that left several sailors and natives dead. On his map, Janszoon gave the place the inauspicious name Cape Keerweer – Dutch for 'turn around'.

Janszoon's encounter is emblematic of the journeys undertaken by European explorers during the so-called Age of Exploration, a period spanning from the 15th to the 17th century. If we are to believe from the name that the intention of such explorers was one of virtuous curiosity, a simple yearning to chart unexplored lands in the name of benevolent empires, then history presents another tale.

Australia was, to the chagrin of early European explorers, not *Terra nullius*, the blank, uninhabited space that filled their maps. The Aboriginal place names, which had been preserved through oral tradition for some 50,000 years, were not only topographic identifiers, but also stories of creation and mythology intertwined with the landscape. It was not with maps that Aboriginals once navigated, but songs. By reciting the songs of ancient creation myths in the correct sequence, one was able to travel vast distances across the land. After European invasion, songs and names were lost. Places were renamed, now reflecting a new kind of story; one of territorial conquest and colonial expeditions, a landscape recalling not mythical deities and spirits, but explorers, geologists, royalty and celebrities.

I came to learn that the study of place names is called toponymy, itself an obscure branch of onomastics – the study of names in general. Toponyms function as both identifiers and monuments, and this was especially true in the days of colonial exploration. Many of the sad toponyms in this book originate from the Age of Exploration; not the kind of exploration we associate with stories of adventure and romance, but a desire to conquer the world, to extract natural resources, expand kingdoms and empires, to exploit and Christianize uncultured and savage peoples. It is not by coincidence that the majority of sad places are to be found in post-colonial countries: North and South America, Canada, Australia, New Zealand. The sadness that Lévi-Strauss discovered in the tropics was a vestige of the slow-burning destruction from the Age of Exploration. What he witnessed was the sadness of disappearing civilizations, a dying world, heavy with the post-colonial melancholy that his subjects were forced to bear.

The first toponymists were storytellers, those who attempted to explain the forgotten origin of place names through a weaving of history, myth and imagination. Landscape often functions as a metaphor for language, and it is said that one can read the landscape as they do a book. In that sense, these place names function as a kind of index; each name the title of a story written across the pages of the landscape. 'From the names might be known how here one man hoped and struggled,' writes George R. Stewart in *Names on the Land*, 'how there another dreamed, or died, or sought fortune, and another joked, twisting an old name to make a new one… they were closely bound with the land itself and the adventures of the people.'

Behind each place name there exists a story, and in the case of these sad places, behind the story a tragic event. And while that is often true, more often the memory of that event fades, and like a weathered signpost that points to a disused path, only the name remains, echoing a time immemorial. In this book, I have attempted to follow those paths. Frequently they wind and fork, splitting into smaller paths, leading to wildly disorienting forests where it becomes impossible to separate history from mythology, fiction from fact and memory from imagination. And so this book is also a journey of unlikely digressions, paths that lead to strange and obscure histories: Soviet science fiction and religious hermits, atomic test sites and death in hotels, the uncanniness of gas stations and the melancholy of the Anthropocene.

I have not been to, nor is it likely I will visit, any of the places in this book. While it can be read as a kind of toponymic collection, it can also be read as a travel guide, or perhaps more accurately, an anti-travel guide; a directory for the crestfallen among us, those inflicted with the black bile of melancholia. In the way that landscape can function as a metaphor for language, the opposite is also true. Stories are also a form of imaginary travel, a way of traversing the landscape of the mind. In Lévi-Strauss's travel book, he attempts to convince the reader not to travel, instead reminiscing about, '...the days of real journeys, when it was still possible to see the full splendour of a spectacle that had not yet been blighted, polluted and spoilt...' He writes with misanthropic despair that, 'The first thing we see as we travel round the world is our own filth, thrown into the face of mankind...' And with that he asks the reader to consider, '...what else can the so-called escapism of travelling do than confront us with the more unfortunate aspects of our history?'

In 1790, the French writer Xavier de Maistre was imprisoned for forty-two days in his bedroom as punishment for duelling. In his room, a mere thirty-six paces, de Maistre relieves his boredom by writing a travel book titled *A Journey Around My Room*. He spends his days traversing the miniscule space as if it were a vast continent, exploring the room's nooks and corners as if they were a boundless wilderness, studying his furniture as if he were an anthropologist, gazing from his window as if he were on an endless train journey crossing strange lands. This form of travel and exploration he recommends to everyone, especially to the poor, the infirm and the lazy, as it is both highly affordable and universally accessible. His imagination transports him far beyond the walls of his room, a journey which he embarks upon with the greatest of exploratory fervour.

De Maistre demonstrates that through stories we can explore and traverse the topographies of the world, without even needing to leave the comfort of our room. 'When I travel through my room,' he writes, 'I rarely follow a straight line: I go from the table towards a picture hanging in a corner; from there, I set out obliquely towards the door; but even though, when I begin, it really is my intention to go there, if I happen to meet my armchair en route, I don't think twice about it, and settle down in it without further ado.'

So I invite you to stay at home, make a cup of tea and settle into your armchair. You're about to explore the saddest places on earth.

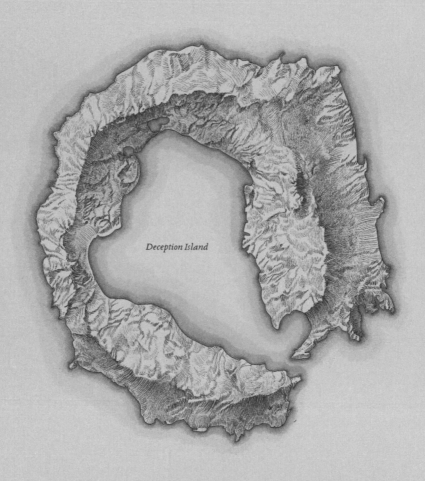

Deception Island

• 62°58 37 S
• 60°39 00 W

Deception Island, Antarctica

DECEPTION IS NO ordinary island. On 22 December 1908, after six days of surging Antarctic storms and crippling seasickness, the crew of the *Pour-quoi-Pas* finally lurched into the steaming caldera of the volcano that is Deception Island. The 12-kilometre-wide amphitheatre of black mountains encircling the port set the stage for a hellish spectacle. Whaling ships – run not on coal but on dead penguins – crowded the bay like a gruesome flotilla carnival. 'Pieces of whale float about on all sides,' Jean-Baptiste Charcot later wrote in his diary from the *Pourquoi-Pas,* '…bodies in the process of being cut up or waiting for their turn alongside the various boats. The smell was unbearable.' Along the blood-soaked beaches of Whalers Bay, among the putrid carcasses and dismembered skeletons, stood enormous iron tanks in which flesh and bone were boiled under roaring furnaces that illuminated the island day and night. Beneath the hulls of the floating slaughterhouses, the blood-tainted caldera bubbled and gurgled, rising into a thick mist that shrouded the scene with a stench of death that hovered over everything. On the beach, alchemists transformed flesh and blubber into oil, and oil into commodity.

It was a 21-year-old Connecticutian by the name of Nathaniel Palmer who, in a sloop barely longer than a rowboat, chanced upon a narrow gap on the island's mountainous side in 1821. At that moment, he had simultaneously discovered both a dozing volcano and, ironically, Antarctica's safest harbour – a rare haven from the furious South Atlantic winds and crushing ice floes.

It wasn't whales he was searching for, but seals. In the Antarctic, fur seals were the first animals to be hunted – and in the most unsustainable fashion imaginable. After being either clubbed or lanced to death, their skins were washed and packed into barrels before being shipped to Europe, North America and China. As more hunters arrived each summer, competition for new hunting grounds became fierce. After only five summers, fur seal populations were decimated and the species was balancing on the verge of extinction. 'After the seals failed,' remarked one commentator (blaming not the hunters but the seals for presumably failing to repopulate fast enough), '…our ships rapidly secured the lead in the whale fishery.' Antarctica offered an abundance of whales and whalers found a global market hungry for their precious oil.

Product label for Seattle Soap Company's Whale Oil Soap.

It is difficult today to appreciate the extent to which Western society depended on whale oil during recent centuries. An ingredient in cosmetics, engine oil and detergents, it also found a role in the production of textiles, jute, leather, linoleum, rope, varnish, paint, soap and margarine. It lubricated the delicate mechanisms of clocks and chronometers, was consumed as a vitamin and became essential in the manufacturing of nitroglycerin for explosives in both world wars. It was, however, in lighting that it found its greatest function. Known as spermaceti – superior to both beeswax and animal tallow for its capacity to produce a brighter, cleaner, smokeless flame – it was bailed out in buckets from the severed heads of sperm whales. Spermaceti lit millions of homes, street lamps, lighthouses and buildings across Europe and North America. Whale oil had become the essential ingredient in the lifeblood of modernity, running through the veins of the new industrial world in order to keep clocks ticking, lights glowing and bombs exploding.

Almost overnight Deception Island was transformed into a bustling whaling factory. The invention of kerosene in the mid-1850s eventually began to replace whale oil as the preferred type of fuel. During the 1920s, whaling ships arrived in Antarctica featuring built-in slipways that allowed whales to be hauled onto the decks for processing, rendering sheltered harbours like Deception unnecessary. Faster processing equalled more oil, in turn generating greater profits, eventually leading to an oversaturated whale oil market. The result was a dramatic fall in oil prices and, as a result, the practice of less-profitable, land-based whale processing abruptly ended. The 19th and 20th centuries' reliance on whale oil draws an uncanny parallel with the 21st century's dependence on mineral oil in more ways than one. 'The whaler was a kind of pirate miner – an excavator of oceanic oil,' writes Philip Hoare in *Leviathan or, The Whale*,

'…stoking the furnace of the Industrial Revolution as much as any man digging coal out of the earth. Whale oil and whalebone were commodities for the Machine Age…' By 1931 the last whaling company on Deception finally ceased operation, ending commercial whaling on the island entirely.

Deception remained abandoned until 1941 when the British Navy decided to make the island less attractive to the German Navy by destroying the remaining oil tanks and other supplies. The Germans failed to show. Argentina, however, visited the following year, leaving a couple of national signs and flags around in a half-hearted attempt to declare sovereignty. Shortly after, the British returned and replaced the flags with their own. In 1944, a group of British scientists established a permanent research station. In 1955, Chile decided that it also wanted a piece of Deception, building its own research station next to the British. While numerous countries simultaneously declared sovereignty over Deception, there was surprisingly little conflict, even reports of tea parties. However, by the end of the 1960s, Deception decided to evict its undesirable occupants with a series of eruptions that destroyed the research stations and buried everything under several feet of mud and ash.

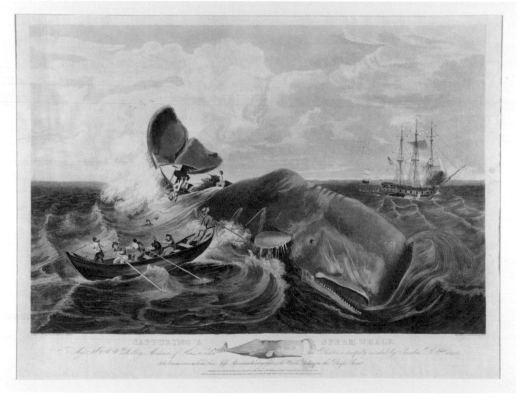

Capturing a Sperm Whale, John William Hill (1835).

Today the island is administered under the Antarctic Treaty System and during the short summers, tourists armed with cameras can be seen wandering through the ruined structures that lean – partially sunken – in the black volcanic sand. William Hazlitt, the English literary critic and philosopher, once wrote, 'Life is the art of being well deceived; and in order that the deception may succeed it must be habitual and uninterrupted.' In 2007, a luxury cruise ship struck rocks as it entered the flooded caldera of Deception Island, spilling 200 gallons of oil and fuel into the bay, and once again the bubbling waters changed colour, this time not red, but black with the new blood of modernity.

End of the World

• 36°34 43 N
• 118°17 31 W

End of the World, California, USA

THE END OF the World is remarkably hard to find. It isn't in the Arctic, or the Antarctic, nor in an ancient Mayan temple or in the Southern Ocean where lost sailors tumble into a mysterious abyss. It can, however, be found tucked away in the recesses of the remote wilderness of eastern California. There, strewn unceremoniously across the vast, unforgiving landscape of the Sierra Nevada mountains, lies the scattered debris of once hopeful gold prospectors.

On 24 January 1848, a mill worker happened upon several glittering yellow flakes in the sand of the American River, a meandering waterway that snakes out from the base of the Sierra Nevada mountains. Little did he know that his chance encounter with those few lustrous specks would alter the course of world history. The *New York Herald* soon caught wind of the finding and, almost overnight, thousands desperate to ensure their fortune were flocking to the California mountains, coming from across North and South America, Europe and even as far away as Australia, New Zealand and China. The word 'California' became indelibly synonymous with gold. The California Dream ensnared itself in the collective imagination, a promised land of wealth and new beginnings. But the dream was only to be realized by those who could first get there. In 1848, there was no easy way to get to California, not even for those already on the continent. America was, for the most part, a vastly unexplored landscape lacking in roads and railway networks. Getting from the east to the west coast by land was a difficult and perilous journey, one that took many months, if the traveller was to even arrive there at all. Paradoxically, most who travelled from the east coast to the west coast did so by sea, sailing all the way around the tip of South America – an arduous voyage that involved eight months of toil. Some sailed south to Panama where, with the aid of canoes and mules, they trekked west through dense tropical jungle, only to board another ship destined for San Francisco once they arrived on the Pacific side. Each route came with its own deadly hazards; from the cataclysmic – shipwrecks, typhoid or cholera, surprise attacks from Natives, robbery by armed gangs – to the more mundane misfortunes, like getting lost en route.

A sailing card for the clipper ship *California*, depicting scenes from the California Gold Rush.

The gold laboured from the earth began to transform the landscape it had emerged from. Towns, and roads connecting them, materialized overnight. To support the many thousands of new arrivals stricken with gold fever, entire industries emerged. The tiny port town of San Francisco, which in 1846 had a mere 200 residents, by 1852 had exploded into a thriving metropolis of 36,000 inhabitants. Gold, and the potent allure of the dreams it fostered, became the alchemical ingredient that transformed wilderness into towns and towns into cities.

In search of the elusive mineral, prospectors roamed out into uncharted lands, prowling further and further into the depths of the Californian wilderness. They scoured riverbeds, cut deep into the mountainsides and overturned stone and earth. They had no maps because they didn't need any – this part of the world was *terra incognita*. The prospectors became explorers. As they colonized the landscape, they christened it with names that reflected their experiences. Places with names such as Last Chance, Devil's Peak, Hell Hole Reservoir, Devil's Gate, Lost Canyon, Deadwood and End of the World go some way to summarizing the grim existence of Californian prospectors. Gold prospecting proved a dangerous gamble that captured the imaginations of many, but rarely paid off. While it occasionally made poor men rich, the vast majority of miners became only poorer. Yet, poverty was the least of their worries, as for the many thousands who had managed to survive their arduous journeys from across the world, death remained their constant companion. The possibility of death from falling rocks, bears, disease, arrows or drowning haunted them like a malicious shadow.

It was not only unfortunate prospectors who suffered from the allure of gold. Both mining and the miners brought devastation to the Native Americans; a race of people who had already endured immeasurable suffering from disease and slaughter at the hands of the Spanish. In California, gold-hungry prospectors drove the Natives from their hunting, fishing and food-gathering lands. Some, in a desperate attempt to protect their homes and families, attacked the miners, only giving the miners justification to massacre entire villages. California's first governor, Peter Burnett, declared that the Natives had two options – extermination or removal. Some 4,000 Native children were sold to settlers as slaves. In 1845, three years before the beginning of the Gold Rush, there were an estimated 150,000 Natives in California. By 1870, only 30,000 remained.

In their indefatigable lust for riches, gold-hungry miners tore open the land, hollowed it out and left it scorched and defiled. Enormous water cannons ripped open mountainsides, rivers were diverted and dammed, entire forests – including thousand-year-old giant sequoia – were logged and poisonous by-products, namely mercury, flowed down rivers and streams, killing fish and rendering the water toxic for centuries to come. The California grizzly bear perhaps fared worst of all animals. To amuse the entertainment-deprived miners, bears were captured and released into gladiatorial rings to battle against bulls and other unsuspecting creatures. When bulls versus bears had grown uninteresting, wealthy miners imported African lions to rejuvenate the excitement. Less than

seventy-five years after the first prospectors headed into the California mountains, almost every California grizzly had been killed. The species was declared extinct in 1922.

Then, one day, the California Gold Rush ended, almost as quickly as it had begun. Thousands, unaware of this news, continued to pour into the already plundered gold fields, only to find there was nothing left. 'Happy days are past,' went one Gold Rush melody. 'The mines have failed at last… There's nothing left for me / I'll never, never see / My happy, happy home so far away.'

During the long Californian summers, tourists wander among the scattered ruins of the Gold Rush era, through a landscape still pockmarked by the trauma of the past. Hollow mines, collapsed buildings, overgrown roads and entire ghost towns now exist only as decaying memories, topographic scars yet to heal. While thousands were murdered, landscapes annihilated, rivers poisoned and species driven to extinction, many look back at the fanatic hunt for that lustrous yellow mineral through rose-coloured glasses. Those who journeyed to the End of the World were part of the largest mass migration in North American history, but for those who were native to the land, the migrants brought little more than misery and destruction.

Grief Bay

Sorrow Islands

• 51° 24' 52.1" N,
• 127° 55' 10.5" W

Sorrow Islands, British Columbia, Canada

LONDON, 1854. The city was in the throes of yet another plague outbreak, a succession of deadly waves that, since 1831, had devastated the city's impoverished population. In just the previous year, the enigmatic illness had killed more than 10,000 people in London and Newcastle alone. In late summer of 1854, the illness again swept through London, this time striking Soho the hardest. In the first three days of September, it killed 127 people. As with the bubonic plague of 1666, people fled to the country, leaving an empty and destitute city in their wake.

For as long as living memory, a perpetual dry haze had hung over London, a persistent grey fog of noxious vapour that poured from coal fires, beer breweries, soap boilers and lime burners. 'It looks partly as if it were made of poisonous smoke,' wrote John Ruskin in his diary, 'very possibly it may be... But mere smoke would not blow to and fro in that wild way. It looks more to me as if it were made of dead men's souls.'

A crusty layer of black soot and filth clung to every surface of the city like barnacles to the bottom of a ship. Under the sweltering summer sun, the Thames had become a simmering cesspool of human and animal faeces, producing an odour so unbearable that the government was forced to dump a concoction of chloride, chalk lime and carbolic acid into it in an attempt to ease the stench. But even the malodorous river failed to compare to the inescapable odour of death that seemed to inhabit the very pores of the city. Blame for the mystery illness inevitably fell on the air itself, which in the collective imagination had become so heavily putrefied, that it had seemingly metamorphosed into a shape-shifting and malicious entity. What made this entity so terrifying was the way it came for some but, inexplicably, spared others. It was a waking nightmare that consumed the imagination of the city, a force so elusive that it could not be hunted or stopped. Robert Seymour, an artist living in London at the time, published in a London newspaper an illustration of an enormous skeleton cloaked in a white sheet hovering over London. Its long, bony arms are outstretched as it glides across the skyline, shrouded in an ominous dark fog. Unable to fight it, all they could do was give it a name. They called it 'miasma'. It was when darkness had rolled over the city that the miasma was believed to emerge, winding its way through the city streets. Those who dared venture outside or neglected to adequately seal their houses had little chance of escaping its clutches. It was in this city that Daniel Pender, a surveyor with the Royal British Navy, lived with his wife and two young daughters. Little is known of Pender, except that while on duty aboard the *Renard* docked in Falmouth, he received word of the ill health of his family back in London. He immediately returned to the city, but by the time he reached it only a day later, he found himself a husband and father no more.

Another man living in London, a physician named John Snow had, to much scepticism, developed an alternative theory about the mystery epidemic. On 8 September 1854, he removed the handle from a communal water pump in Soho and, almost immediately, the plague in that neighbourhood came to an end. It would, however, be several more months before the culprit was identified; not a malevolent vapour as many had believed, but Asiatic cholera spread not through the air, but the city's drinking water.

For Daniel Pender, however, it was already too late. With the haste of one who had been absolved of all things that bind one to a place, he left London and returned to the sea. Three years had passed and, still haunted by his grief, Pender found himself in charge of surveying the vast coast of British Columbia. His task was to systematically map and name the uncharted wilderness of the new country's expansive coastline.

Death rowing on a putrid Thames surrounded by miasma. Illustration from *The London Charivari* magazine, 1858.

From 1857 to 1870, he surveyed and named mountains, bays, islands, channels, rivers and inlets; features of a landscape that, until then, had only been vague entities on existing maps. It was through this incantatory process that Pender came to discover the act of naming as both a combatant to the transience of memory and a remedy to the grief of his past. In 1863, he was promoted to captain of the ship *Devastation*, after which he named Devastation Channel. For other names, Pender drew inspiration from his earlier life. A small group of islands off Vancouver Island's west coast he named after characters from Charles Dickens's novel *Dombey and Son*.

A B R A C A D A B R A
A B R A C A D A B R
A B R A C A D A B
A B R A C A D A
A B R A C A D
A B R A C A
A B R A C
A B R A
A B R
A B
A

Abracadabra in the form of a descending triangle.

During the 1666 Great Plague of London, it was common practice to inscribe the word 'abracadabra' in the form of a descending triangle on the front door of one's house. Before its inseparable association with stage magic, the word was believed to possess the mystical quality of protection. It was Quintus Serenus Sammonicus, a physician in the 3rd century AD, who first prescribed the word abracadabra as a preventative to ward off illness and disease. Yet, its origins can be traced back even further to the ancient Aramaic language in which it means, 'I create what I speak'. The notion of a word or a name possessing esoteric qualities can also be found in the German fairy tale *Rumpelstiltskin*, in which the miller's daughter has to guess the dwarf's name in order to keep her child. Both instances suggest that names can be more than identifiers; they can also act as both protectors and saviours. Sorrow and Grief are names that Pender used to transform a landscape into a story, one that could be read and navigated, and also left behind.

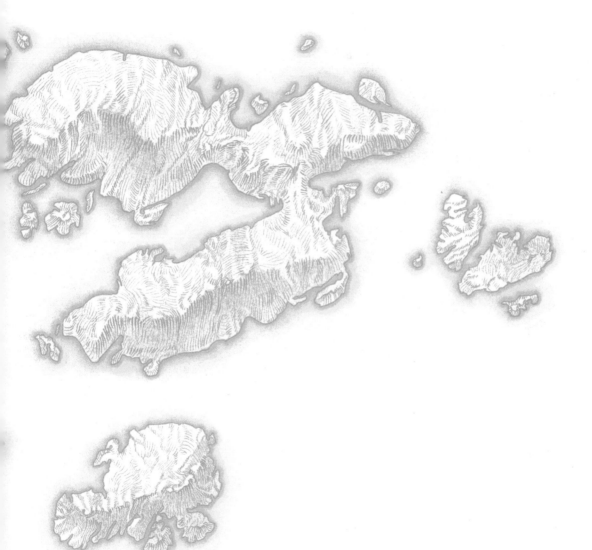

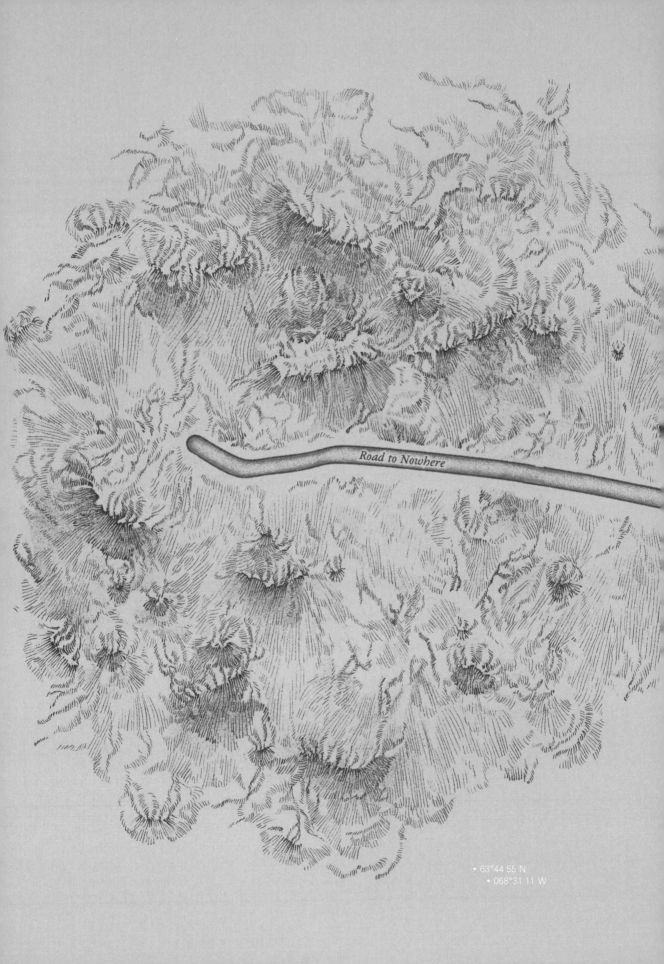

Road to Nowhere

• 63°44 55 N
• 068°31 11 W

Road to Nowhere, Iqaluit, Canada

A SLIGHTLY BENT AND rusted pole inauspiciously marks the beginning of the road. The sign, which one can only assume once indicated the road's name, has long disappeared. The narrow dirt road snakes around a low-slung hill and past a cluster of recently built timber apartment blocks. Painted in stark primary colours, the buildings appear like gaudy illustrations from a colouring-in book, set against the bleached Arctic landscape. Off to the right of the road lies the body of water that is Dead Dog Lake. Through an undulating, treeless terrain of either (depending on the season) deep snow or Arctic tundra, the road eventually melts into the surrounding landscape before coming to an abrupt end. At this point, one expects to find Nowhere, but instead discovers a rusted gate to an abandoned shooting range.

The Road to Nowhere can be found on the outskirts of Iqaluit. The smallest of the Canadian capitals, Iqaluit lies along the frozen coastline in the far north-east of the country. Geographically closer to the capital of Greenland than Canada, it's also the only main city not connected to the rest of the country by road, rail or, for most of the year, ship. It's a city quite literally in the middle of nowhere, with at least one road that actually goes to nowhere. Curiously, despite its isolation, it's also Canada's fastest growing capital city. Until recently, Iqaluit was little more than an insignificant coastal village inhabited by a handful of Inuit fishermen. However, everything changed during the Second World War when, unannounced, the American Air Force constructed a secret airbase on the town's outskirts. Going by the codename Crystal Two, the airbase formed part of the Crimson Route, a series of American and Canadian convoy lines used for transporting air supplies from North America to the raging war in Europe. Almost overnight, this tiny Arctic fishing village was transformed into a bustling military operation, inhabited by hundreds of builders, and administration and military staff. By the war's end, it had grown to become a small city of over a thousand permanent residents. Then, between 1959 and 1962, during the height of America's fears of the Soviet Union, the North American Aerospace Defense Command (known as

NORAD) built a collection of secret radar stations on the city's outskirts. They were among the hundreds that secretly stretched across the Arctic, from the Pacific to the Atlantic. The invisible line of defence spanned nearly 10,000 kilometres, from Alaska to Iceland. Its purpose was to detect and thwart the Soviet bombers and warships en route to America, for an invasion that many believed was imminent.

It's difficult now to imagine the perpetual state of fear that possessed the collective imagination of America during the 1950s and early 1960s. Air-raid sirens were installed in countless towns and cities. Bunkers were built under schools, shops and government buildings. In homes, TV screens blazed with images of cataclysmic mushroom clouds consuming unsuspecting landscapes. In the suburbs, middle-class families built backyard fallout shelters stocked with cans of beans and Spam. In schools, children rehearsed putting on gas masks. Spared the vast political complexities of nuclear warfare, children were instead introduced to Bert, the anthropomorphic cartoon turtle, who demonstrated how to dive for cover under flimsy wooden school desks. 'Bert the Turtle was very alert,' went the catchy tune of the Civil Defense propaganda film, '… when danger threatened him he never got hurt, he knew just what to do… He'd duck! And cover! Duck! And cover!' When, on 30 October 1961, the Soviets dropped the 50-megaton Tsar Bomba over a remote Arctic

archipelago – unleashing an annihilating force 1,570 times that which collectively flattened Hiroshima and Nagasaki – it became apparent that Bert the Turtle needed better advice.

A poster for Bert the Turtle from the Federal Civil Defense Administration (1951).

On several nerve-racking occasions during the Cold War, the American government came disturbingly close to throwing the world back into the early Stone Age. One such near-apocalyptic incident happened on 24 November 1961, when communication lines between the US Strategic Air Command and several NORAD radar stations in the Arctic suddenly and inexplicably went dead. The simultaneous loss of communications from these stations made little sense; numerous fail-safe measures had been put in place to prevent such an accidental loss of signal. In a colossal rush to judgement, it was assumed that everyone's worst fear had materialized and a full-scale Soviet nuclear attack was underway. Air force and missile bases across the United States went on red alert; B-52 bombers loaded with nuclear warheads rolled out onto runways ready for take-off. For twelve excruciating minutes, everyone stood with collectively held breath, awaiting orders for a counter-attack. However, just before any orders were given, someone discovered that the communication lines ran through a single telephone relay station in Colorado and that during the night a motor had overheated, shutting down lines between the radar stations and trigger-happy commanders who rested trembling fingers on large red buttons.

As we know, the Soviets never arrived and the bombs never fell. Fallout shelters around the country became wine cellars, rations expired, gas masks became souvenirs and Bert the Turtle was unceremoniously retired from civil duty. Over time, the communist fear subsided and faded from memory. The Arctic radar stations also fell into redundancy, eventually becoming replaced with newer forms of satellite technology. However, many still remain, dotted across the snow-covered landscapes of the north in their abandonment, now merely archaic symbols of redundant warfare. If you find yourself on the outskirts of Iqaluit, at the very end of the Road to Nowhere, it's possible to look north, across the undulations of tundra marsh and swamp lakes, and in the distance see the white mushroom domes of one particular NORAD radar station. It is a relic of history, a derelict monument of one road that, quite fortunately, led to nowhere.

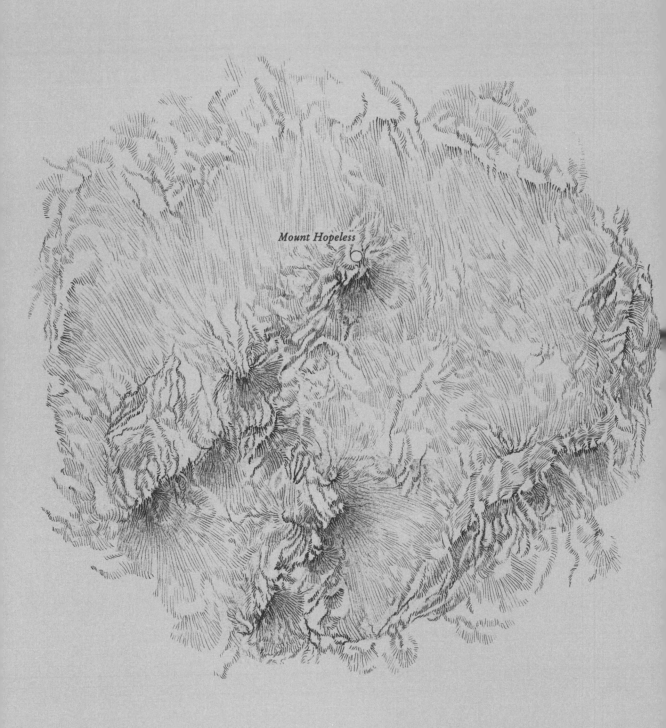

Mount Hopeless

• 34°01 S
  • 150°03 E

Mount Hopeless, South Australia, Australia

IN A REMOTE part of the South Australian outback, a mound of stones creeps above an otherwise featureless landscape. It was here on 2 September 1840 that Edward Eyre stood with a sinking heart. In every direction except whence he had come, a glistening lake of saltwater touched the horizon. Eyre's expedition was not going as planned.

Ever since Europeans first arrived on the continent some seventy years earlier, rumours had abounded over what untold mysteries lay at the island's vast interior. Some speculated about an inland sea or an immense river network, while others envisioned lush pastoral lands. It was easy to make unsubstantiated claims; as no European had yet ventured very far from the coast, one was unlikely to have even their wildest speculations refuted. In 1827, Thomas Maslen, a retired British East India Company officer, published a book titled *Friend of Australia*. While Maslen himself had not even been to Australia, he saw that as no obstacle to producing his very own explorer's handbook, complete with maps and instructions for those hoping to venture into the island's mysterious interior. Perhaps the grandest claim the book made was that an enormous inland sea filled the centre of the continent, one that connected to the Indian Ocean by a vast delta. Maslen had even drafted an illustrated map. 'It is impossible to contemplate,' he wrote, 'the works of a Bounteous Creator, and believe that any imperfections can exist on the face of our planet, which would certainly be the case if such a continent had no outlet of its waters.' Maslen assumed that as North America had the Mississippi, South America the Amazon, Africa the Nile and Asia the Ganges and Mekong, it simply made sense that his Bounteous Creator would also gift Australia its own major river system – even one flowing into an inland sea. So convinced was Maslen about his inland sea that he insisted any legitimate inland explorer would be wise to bring a fleet of boats

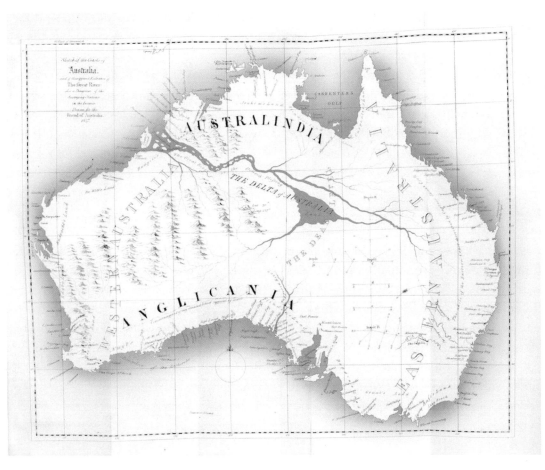

The erroneous map of Australia's inland sea included in Thomas Maslen's book, *Friend of Australia*, 1827.
Image courtesy of Hordern House Rare Books, Sydney.

with them. The book proved successful, not in sales or useful information, but in fuelling the inland sea mythology.

It was ten years later that the scrawny, pale-faced and soft-spoken 23-year-old Edward Eyre decided to settle the matter once and for all. He had travelled to Australia as a way of avoiding the military, university and his nagging parents back in England. Above all else, he wanted to be an explorer, and where better to fulfil that dream than the newly discovered island of *Terra Incognita*. After arriving and failing at sheep farming, he drove his flock to the newly formed township of Adelaide where he sold them for what amounted to a small fortune. It was with these funds that he could now realize his adventurous fantasies. On 18 June 1840, with a team of five European men, Eyre's close friends John Baxter and Wylie, two Aboriginal guides, thirteen horses, forty sheep and three months of supplies, Eyre set off from Adelaide straight for the continent's uncharted interior.

After three months, the team found themselves surrounded not by lush pastoral lands, but by a landscape, '…bare, destitute of vegetation, and thickly coated in salt, presenting the most miserable and melancholy aspect imaginable'. Eyre climbed a mountain of stones and, in a state of utter despondence, peered out over an impassable liquid landscape.

He had indeed found a large body of water, but it was too close to Adelaide and clearly not the mythical inland sea. 'Ascended Mount Hopeless,' wrote Eyre in his diary, unintentionally christening a mountain in the process. 'Cheerless and hopeless indeed was the prospect before us. This has closed all my dreams for the expedition, and put an end to the undertaking from which so much was anticipated. I had now a view before me that would have damped the ardour of the most enthusiastic, or dissipated the doubts of the most sceptical.'

Unfortunately, Eyre's expedition would only get worse. After abandoning any hope of discovering the interior, the party trekked back to Adelaide, resupplied, then set off again, this time south-west along the uncharted coastline. For two months, they marched westward under the blazing desert sun. To their left, sheer cliffs fell into a surging ocean; to their right, an endless expanse of hostile desert.

Their only option was to march ahead or retreat once more in shame. No doubt feeling responsible for the unfolding calamity, Eyre ordered most of his party back to Adelaide and continued on with just Baxter, Wylie and two Aboriginal guides. As weeks turned into months, the expedition became an exercise in survival. They dug holes in search of water and licked the morning dew from desert shrubs. Sheep and horses perished. Supplies were abandoned. Occasionally, they encountered Aboriginal tribesmen who took pity on the pathetic group, showing them where to find water. Just when it seemed as if things could not have gotten worse, one evening the two guides snatched much of the camp's remaining supplies, killed John Baxter and fled into the desert. Eyre was devastated. He and Wylie had neither food nor water. Yet the two men continued their futile march in the searing heat, towards almost certain death.

Some days later, they stumbled across the rotting carcass of a horse, which, out of sheer desperation, they dined upon – unsurprisingly, almost killing themselves in the process. One day, almost a year into their dismal expedition, on the verge of starvation, they spotted a ship anchored just off the coast. The men scrambled down the cliff and, shortly after, found themselves on the French whaling vessel *Mississippi*. While the sailors took pity on the famished men, they could only give them a few supplies and soon sent them back on their frivolous way.

More than a year after leaving Adelaide, the two emaciated men one day walked into the small coastal town of Albany. They had trekked some 2,500 kilometres, the distance from London to Moscow. Their journey had taught them many things: how to find water in the desert, that one should not eat decaying animals; and they had certainly gotten much exercise and a radiant tan, but, after everything, what lay at the country's interior still remained a mystery. Eyre's expedition also failed to provide any revelatory insights into the country's vast topography. Perhaps, almost ironically, it would be the salt lake, the very lake that forecast doom for Eyre's expedition, that he would lend his name to and be remembered for. Edward Eyre returned to Adelaide; weary, skinny and completely devoid of yearning for any further exploratory adventures.

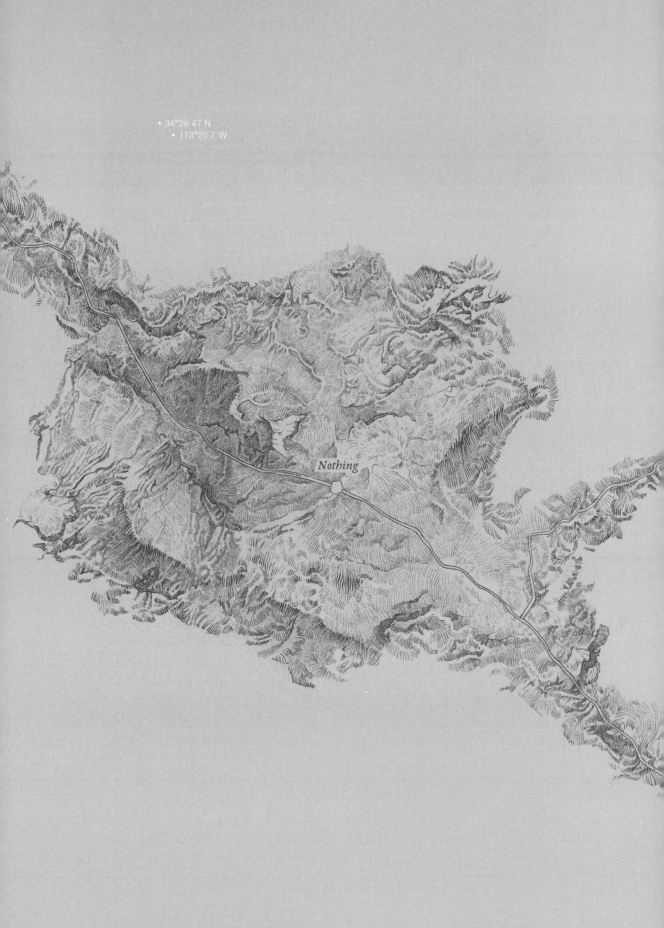

34°28 47 N
113°20 7 W

Nothing

Nothing, Arizona, USA

I T SEEMS FITTING that Nothing is a ghost town. In the brittle heat of the Arizona desert, along a lonesome stretch of Route 93 somewhere between Las Vegas and Phoenix, the desert heat and wind slowly erode the town's decaying structures back into oblivion. One attempting to describe the town must do so in the way one takes a photograph – capturing a single moment in constant flux, a process of perpetual decay like the melting of Antarctic glaciers.

At this moment, a sand-white gas station leans in stiff rebellion to gravity with the words 'NO TRESPASSING' scrawled in black spray paint across two windows. The satirically named and completely empty 'All-Mart' is surrounded by random scatterings of ornamental garbage; the skeleton of a sofa, beer bottles and floral underwear – the kind that always seems to mysteriously appear in such places. Perhaps most curious is the concrete foundation of what was once the Nothing Rock Shop, a wonderfully desperate attempt to turn one of the few freely available resources of the Arizona desert into desirable roadside souvenirs. The double sentence declaration of the town sign begins, 'The staunch citizens of Nothing are full of Hope, Faith, and Believe in the work ethic.' Without warning, it takes a sharp nihilistic U-turn, shifting from present to past tense, both contradicting the previous statement and imposing a scene of hopeless resignation: 'Thru-the-years-these dedicated people had faith in Nothing, hoped for Nothing, worked at Nothing, for Nothing.'

The American desert; a magical frontier and fantasy playground where secret military technologies are tested, UFOs buzz the sky, atomic bombs are detonated and the socially disillusioned retreat to reinvent themselves. Nothing was an unlikely experiment in urban development. Founded in 1977, it was Arizona's smallest town. During its brief economic boom in the early 1980s, the population swelled to a total of four. Here, passers-by could stop for all their gas, grocery and mineral needs. Apart from occasional truckers, vacuum-cleaner salesmen and lost vacationers, Nothing's daring location drew the business of a special kind of traveller: the migratory 'snowbird' – a term referring to retirees who travel south for the duration of the winter in their nomadic homes known as recreational vehicles – RVs. Historically, Florida was the preferred snowbird destination, but several

The former Nothing Rock Shop.
Image courtesy of Aaron Wood.

other temperate southern states have seen the emergence of RV seasonal cities. Just 120 miles south of Nothing, one may witness the largest gathering of snowbirds in North America: the immense spectacle that is the RV city of Quartzsite. Many thousands flock each winter to form a community – bizarre as it is temporary – of retirees who share little more in common than an aversion to cold weather and a desire to be among their fellow RV nomads. By mid-January, some

26,000 vehicles roll in each day. No fewer than 175,000 luxury motor homes, converted vans, school buses and trailers crowd mere inches apart into 79 trailer parks, spilling out seven miles on either side of town. By late summer, Quartzsite becomes a sprawling car park in the desert, a boundless ocean of motor homes, plastic deck chairs, umbrellas and taut leathery skin, all searing under the Arizona sun.

Flea markets are the main attraction in Quartzsite, a bustling economy in the exchange and consumption of useless objects. Curiously, it is not the chainsaw sculpture, imitation African art, shag-pile rugs, thematic windmills or hand-made brooms that are the main market attraction, but rocks. In 1965, the mining town of Quartzsite hosted the 'Pow Wow Rock, Gem & Mineral Show', giving birth to what is now arguably America's greatest annual rock show spectacle. These days, there are some eight major rock and mineral shows and countless vendors hawking an endless array of geological artifacts. Rocks are introduced into the Quartzsite marketplace with the mystical quality of an object that possesses neither function nor value. They act instead as a form of social lubricant, bought and sold not because they are valuable, but precisely because they are worth nothing.

It could be argued that as a noun 'nothing' cannot function, as there is no object to which it refers. A counter-argument, however, might say that 'nothing' is a concept, and concepts are also things, however immaterial. It could be argued that our relationship with the world is the equal act of experiencing absence as well as presence and that terms like 'nothing' simply serve to illustrate this.

In 1958, the artist Yves Klein staged an exhibition at the Iris Clert Gallery in Paris titled *Le Vide* or 'The Void'. An extensive publicity campaign leading up to the exhibition meant that hundreds of fanatical Parisians queued down the street in excited anticipation on the opening night. To heighten the mystery of the exhibition, two Republican Guards in full regalia stood at the gallery's entrance. When the doors finally swung open and people rushed into the gallery, it was not what they saw that shocked them, but what they didn't see – the gallery was entirely empty. Remarkably, the event was an immense success. 'It is frenzied,' Klein remarked at the opening. 'The crowd is so dense that one cannot move anywhere.' It was not the empty gallery that Klein considered as the artwork, but the emptiness inside – the presence of nothing itself. In the gallery space, everything was removed – any manifestation of objects as artworks, manual or skilled labour, or the artist as performer. Complete absence became the point of creation, the logical consequence of art without an artist.

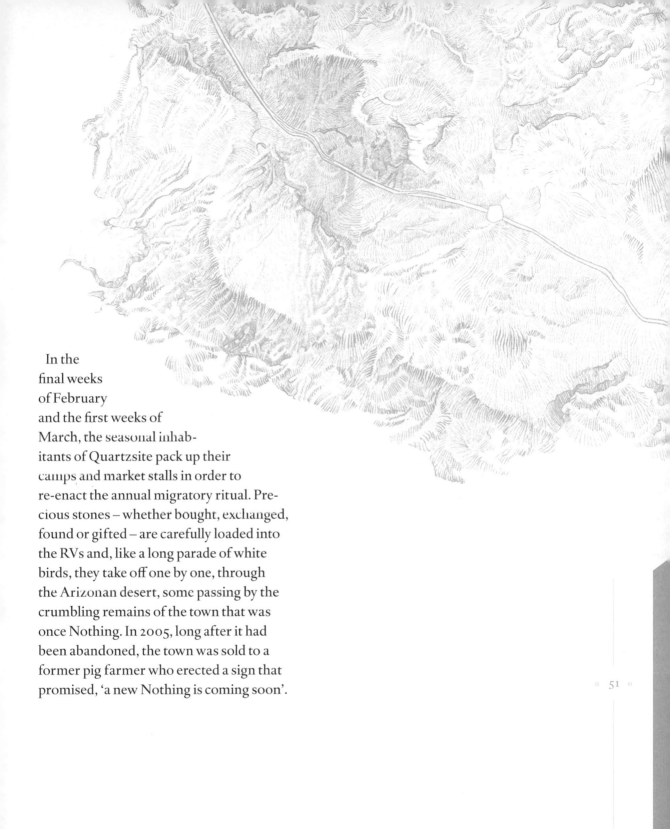

In the
final weeks
of February
and the first weeks of
March, the seasonal inhabitants of Quartzsite pack up their
camps and market stalls in order to
re-enact the annual migratory ritual. Precious stones – whether bought, exchanged,
found or gifted – are carefully loaded into
the RVs and, like a long parade of white
birds, they take off one by one, through
the Arizonan desert, some passing by the
crumbling remains of the town that was
once Nothing. In 2005, long after it had
been abandoned, the town was sold to a
former pig farmer who erected a sign that
promised, 'a new Nothing is coming soon'.

51

Cartographies
of
Space

In Amsterdam, not far from where I live, is the Hotel Prins Hendrik. It was outside this hotel at roughly 3.10am on the morning of 13 May 1988 that the dead body of Chet Baker was found spread out across the sidewalk. For a time, Baker was one of the most celebrated musicians of modern jazz – his haunting trumpet and velvet melancholy voice played across airwaves the world over. He had been staying alone in the hotel room, indulging in a habitual heroin and cocaine binge, when it's assumed he leaned out of the window a little too far. When I ride past the hotel, I occasionally stop and watch tourists taking photographs of the bronze memorial plaque attached to the hotel wall near where his body was found. Selfie-stick-wielding couples often embrace each other in front of the plaque or gaze up with squinted eyes at the window from which Baker tumbled. From time to time visitors can be seen lying on the footpath, posing as the corpse of a drug addicted jazz musician.

The hotel wasted little time in capitalizing on this serendipitous mishap. Serious Chet Baker pilgrims can request room 210 – the room christened by the hotel as the Chet Baker Room. This I know, because I was one of those people. I wanted to stay in room 210 on 13 May, but it was already occupied by a more fanatical Chet Baker pilgrim, so I reluctantly took it a few nights later. I spent the evening sitting alone in the dark, drinking beer and listening to the classic 1954 album *Chet Baker Sings*. Through the window the lights of the city danced, and in that moment I tried unsuccessfully to feel something of what Baker had felt that night in May of 1988. The culmination of the evening arrived at 3.09am. I opened the window and gazed down at the sidewalk, the grey cement still wet from afternoon rain and now littered with cigarette butts. 'The walls of my room fade away in the blue,' sung Chet from the darkened room, 'And I'm deep in a dream of you.'

I left the room key at the unattended front desk and walked out into the quiet night air. Riding home through the sleeping city, I felt content in my small contribution to contemporary myth-making, the enshrinement of a site for future ritual. Lying in bed as morning light illuminated the room, I thought of the pilgrims who will succeed me in the following centuries, returning, year after year, to momentarily bask in the poignancy of lagging memory, seeking a fragment of the immortality that emanates from within the place itself.

A thin silver haze hung across the winding road and the air conditioner clattered like a tumble dryer full of small stones. S. clutched the oversized steering wheel with both hands and stared intently into the distance. The car was an ancient Buick station wagon that was once canary yellow, but had since faded to the colour of stained teeth. It was a relic from the golden age of terrestrial travel, an iconic symbol of the Great American Road Trip. We were in Cape Cod, Massachusetts, looking for the gas station depicted in Edward Hopper's 1940 painting *Gas*.

Hopper, the iconic connoisseur of solitary travel, spent many years on the Cape. He built a summer house in South Truro along a quiet stretch of beach, a base from which he could venture out to seek the lonely intersections of postmodernity, mobility and domestic life. I had spent several nights trawling through blogs, articles and Google Maps, searching for the location of the gas station. One article from the *Boston Globe* dated 4 April 2010 announced that the gas station in question was along Route 6 somewhere south of Truro. It was reportedly in a state of severe dilapidation and under threat of demolition, as no one was interested in its questionable historical value. Years had passed since that article was published, so I decided an urgent pilgrimage to Cape Cod was in order.

'Do you want to take a road trip?' I asked S., luring her with the prospect of regular dips in the ocean and succulent New England lobster.

We had been cruising back and forth along the same stretch of Route 6 for what felt like hours, until we finally decided to ask for directions. We pulled into the empty parking lot of a restaurant named Moby Dick's and went inside. Suspended from every surface were oars, buoys, life vests, anchors, fishnets and innumerable other oceanic paraphernalia. S. was looking on the counter for a bell to ring when a woman appeared from the kitchen. She radiated a ubiquitous New Englander smile and wore an apron smeared with fish guts. We explained our predicament and she seemed sympathetic but unable to help. Another woman materialized, and we again explained what we were looking for. This one seemed to know where our illusive gas station could be found and on a napkin sketched for us a rudimentary map in red pen. We thanked them and promised to return later for dinner. Armed with this archaic technology, I drove while S. navigated, rotating the napkin map in various directions as if it were a broken compass.

I had for some time been thinking about the strange, long-standing preoccupation that many artists have with gas stations. There's Ed Ruscha's iconic 1963 photo series *Twentysix Gasoline Stations*; the first modern artist's book that the Library of Congress famously rejected but now sells for thousands on Amazon. Or Andy Warhol's *Mobilgas* painting from 1985. Or most recently, the fashion photographer David LaChapelle's hallucinatory series *Gas Stations*. Then, of course, there's Hopper, the one who started this curiously persistent artistic meme.

In 1940, when Hopper painted *Gas*, both cars and gas stations were becoming increasingly common sights across the American landscape. Personal mobility was no longer a luxury afforded to the privileged, but now a common right. The station featured in *Gas* is a small, white-timber station that looks more like a quaint farm cottage. Through its open door and windows, yellow light stretches out towards a line of red gas pumps and to the road beyond. During the day, the gas station would probably look homely and inviting – but on the cusp of night, it appears distinctly *unheimlich*. It sits surrounded by a mass of dark, ominous woods. The fading light imparts a dull, shadowless ambience over the scene. The onset of evening and the winding road suggest a place in transition, or a moment of transgression.

It's for good reason that I've always found gas stations disturbing. They are artificial spaces, uncertain arrangements of material and form suspended between *here* and *there*, the real and imaginary. Perhaps it's this quality that makes them so apt for cinema. There's the one from the 1974 film *Texas Chainsaw*

Massacre, which in the movie is fittingly named Last Chance Gas Station – it's still around and has been renamed We Slaughter Barbecue. Or the quaint 1950s seaside gas station in Hitchcock's *The Birds*, where a hapless customer is pecked to death by a gang of deranged seagulls. Perhaps the most terrifying example is to be found in the 1988 Dutch film *The Vanishing*. In the film, young lovers Rex and Saskia drive to France for their summer vacation, but when they stop at a bustling French highway gas station, Saskia goes inside to buy beer and completely vanishes. Rex's search for her starts out as frantic, then turns obsessive. It drags on for years, until Rex finally meets Saskia's kidnapper. The ending is profoundly unsettling; Stanley Kubrick declared it to be the most terrifying film he had ever seen.

Of course it's no coincidence that Saskia disappeared at a gas station. Like cinema itself, gas stations reside in the world of placelessness. They are uncanny islands, sites untethered to either place or memory. While Hopper may have been the first to introduce gas stations to art, S. and I would be the first gas station art pilgrims.

As we approached the thin red X marked on the napkin, my heart slumped into my stomach. S. veered off the road onto a patch of dirt carved out of the surrounding forest. We stepped out into the shadowless midday sun and stood squinting with folded arms. Here was indeed a structure; however, one so thoroughly engaged in the business of ruination that it appeared barely recognizable as having once been a building at all. Its four timber walls and tin roof had imploded like the withered carcass of a popped balloon. A fresh smattering of greenery ornamented the decaying heap.

On the opposite side of the road – a road on which cars drifted by in an endless glinting stream – was a concrete skeleton of a building in the process of being contrived into existence. Two heavily tanned Hispanic men were unloading long plastic pipes from the back of a pick-up. I thought of Robert Smithson, who declared buildings under construction as 'ruins in reverse'. Together we leaned against the front of the car, shading our eyes from the baking sun. We gazed silently at the *mise-en-scène*, trying – as perhaps those in Athens or Rome do – to deduce some meaningful conclusion about the circularity of time, or the triumph of time over history, or as Smithson put it, '…the memory-traces of an abandoned set of futures'.

As we were about to leave, I noticed a For Sale sign nailed to a tree with a phone number written across it. S. called the number and after a series of questions was told that the location was in fact that of a former pizzeria and no, to the real estate agent's knowledge, not that of our mythical gas station. As we got back into the car, S. wasted no time in reminding me of my thus far unfulfilled promise of beach and succulent New England lobster, so we once again drove back south towards Truro. Perhaps it would still be possible, I quietly surmised, to catch a glimpse of Hopper's beach house before the day was out.

While I pretended that I did not want to go to the beach, it was in fact the only thing I wanted to do. Yet if I admitted this, it would imply that this trip to Cape Cod was not a serious research excursion, but a vacation. I would like to attribute my disdain for vacations and vacationers to some high-brow asceticism, but that's not the case. By never being on vacation, it is possible to relieve myself from the unbearable burden of expectation. Never is one so hypersensitive to failed hopes and expectations than while on vacation, for it is during these most anticipated of days that we expect nothing less than a perpetual state of bliss.

My severe allergy to vacation disappointment likely stems from years of overexposure as a child. I recall those much-anticipated family vacations, those brief summer weeks that consisted of one disappointment after another, gradually expanding my family's capacity for disappointment to profound new levels, only, incredibly, to be exceeded the following year. I now find even the slightest suggestion of disappointment utterly unbearable, and much like someone who will die if they touch a peanut, I take extreme precautions to avoid it. I want nothing more than to tell the lonely, dispirited and probably immensely disappointed travellers in Hopper's bleak motels and gloomy diners that the secret is to keep the bar of hope flush to the ground; to expect the very worst from each moment and believe that the next moment will likely be as terrible as the last. And then, I would tell them, your vacation will be a fine and memorable experience.

We pulled into an empty parking lot next to the beach. The ocean was a flat metallic grey that blended seamlessly into the galvanized afternoon sky. S. decided to brave the frigid surf while I, impervious to water that isn't glassy and bath temperature, slipped off my sneakers and strolled south along the firm wet sand at the water's edge.

There is a strange spatial and temporal detachment when walking across a landscape devoid of landmarks. After what could have been one or five miles, I noticed over some rolling dunes the grey peaked roof and white walls of what appeared, based on photos I had seen, to be Hopper's summer house. I clambered over the grassy dunes and approached cautiously. Inside the house was dark and, after I was satisfied that it was unoccupied, I strode up and peered in through a small, web-veiled window next to the side door. The house was empty, not just of people, but of everything. Afternoon sun streamed through a window on the other side of the building, illuminating a golden rectangle of empty space across the timber floor. In a twist of poetic circularity, Hopper's own house had developed its very own Hopper-fied placelessness. It no longer possessed the human presence which gives a place its placeness. Place had returned to space.

Looking through the window, I realized the scene resembled one of Hopper's last paintings, *Sun in an Empty Room*. In the painting, sunlight enters through an open window to the right of the room and spills diagonally across a section of wall and floor. It was painted in 1963, just four years before his death. Both room and painting now appeared as prophecy and memory. Unlike the complex dioramic scenes of Hopper's earlier work, it's as if, after a lifetime of attempts to articulate the essence of solitude and emptiness, he had reduced it into its most concentrated form. It's a scene of absence absolute. Mark Strand comments that *Sun in an Empty Room* is, '…a vision of the world without us; not merely a place that excludes us, but a place emptied of us'.

Hopper's most celebrated paintings are like an entire film compressed into a single frame. From that frame we can elaborate a story, the characters, the narrative arc, how it began and how it will end. Yet *Sun in an Empty Room* is an image without agency or narrative. It's a scene in which the temporal has been compressed to such potency as to obliterate itself. The result is less of cinema, more the kind of hyperawareness afforded by psychedelics, in the way even mundane space – the sunlit corner of an empty room – suddenly emanates its own extraordinary beauty and being.

I returned to the beach and walked until I reached a point where all reminders of civilization had receded from view. Lying in the soft white sand, still warm from the afternoon sun, I stared up through the glacier-blue dome at the first stars littering the sky. Like a skipping record, the waves rolled, folded and collapsed in endless rhythmic succession. And like the waves, I had for the second time that day the impression that time and space itself had also folded and collapsed into a single ongoing moment.

I returned to the parking lot and found S. dozing in the car. When I opened the door and got in, she woke instantly.

'I'm starving,' she said, tugging her seat upright. 'Did you get lost or something?'

We drove into Truro. Even at this early hour the town appeared not just bucolic, but abandoned. Light from empty stores spilled out over empty streets. As we continued north along Route 6, passing quaint, hand-painted timber signs advertising bed and breakfast, sea-view lodging and private cottages, I dismissed them as unappealing, uninviting, or unsightly. (What I implicitly meant, however, was unaffordable.) Until, on the periphery of civilization, I saw in the distance a flickering neon beacon: BREAKWATER MOTEL – CABLE TV – AIR-CONDITIONED – VACANCY. It was the kind of establishment I had been waiting for; an archetypal single-level motel sitting around a central parking lot. It was a relic from another era, the kind of place that seemed to emanate a vague, unidentifiable threat of violence. I immediately announced it as charming and cinematic.

As we entered the overlit haze of the motel lobby, we noticed a fleshy woman sitting behind the counter, her gaze locked on a small flickering TV mounted to the wall in the corner of the room.

'Hi,' said S. 'We're after one room, just for the night.'

The receptionist peeled her eyes from the screen, looked at S, then me, then back to S. With the speed of a deep-sea diver, she turned around and extracted a single key from a wooden drawer. Above us, a ceiling fan turned with the greatest of strain, as if it were not circulating air, but a thick translucent liquid.

She dropped the key into S.'s palm. Attached to the key was a miniature orange life vest.

'Room 6,' she said, slowly shifting her gaze back to the TV. 'Check out is at 10am.'

We found our room and dropped our bags onto the bed, which had clearly seen a lot of mileage, then set out on foot in search of dinner. In America, I relish any opportunity to walk somewhere; a small act of self-righteous defiance towards a nation who insist on driving everywhere, even when it's completely unnecessary to do so. We entered the first restaurant we came to, which is how we found ourselves at the Hot L Bar and Grille. It used to be called the Hotel Bar and Grille, the young waiter informed us with considerable pride as he led us to our table, until one day the 'e' in Hotel blew out on the restaurant's garish neon sign, and, ingeniously, instead of repairing the blown tube, they simply embraced the modified spelling. We were seated by a large window, which afforded a spectacular view of the sign in question. We glanced at the menu before ordering two steamed New England lobsters with fries, a potato salad and a couple of house special, mystery cocktails.

The drone of country music filled the restaurant. A few tables away sat a middle-aged couple in matching denim, the only other people in the restaurant. Their wooden chairs appeared miniature and frail under their bodies. They sat facing each other, arguing about something. S. was using the reflection of a knife to pick something out of her teeth, insouciant to the unfolding drama across the room. 'I ain't doin' it again!' the husband moaned, staring with a petulant expression into the palm of his hand. 'You said you would, Craig,' the woman growled in a low voice. 'We've been over this a *hundred goddamn times*.'

Our waiter arrived with two enormous fluorescent-orange lobsters, sliced down the middle and oozing crustacean juices.

S. gazed at them with wild eyes like an impoverished child. We devoured our food with shameless vehemence, coating every surface in sticky, glistening fluid. We paid the check and, with swollen bellies, waddled painfully back to the motel through the quiet darkness of night.

In front of the room adjacent to ours sat two men smoking cigars and drinking beer. They reclined on folding deck chairs, facing the empty parking lot as if it were the ocean at sunset. Light from the windows of their room illuminated them from behind, obscuring their faces and casting long shadows out into the night.

'Evening,' slurred a voice from out of the darkness.

S. fumbled with the key as if intoxicated. Eventually the door swung open, and she staggered in and collapsed onto the bed. I stood in the doorway searching the wall for a light switch.

'Join us for a beer,' came another voice, devoid of enthusiasm. Before I had time to formulate an excuse, one of the men had gone inside and returned with a folding beach chair. The other man reached into a cooler and extracted a can of Miller Lite, which he cracked open with the stunning grace and the single-handed dexterity of an action refined over many thousands of times. I accepted the wet beer can and took my seat. The three of us sat staring out into the velvet black night. The air was still and sultry, heavy with the odour of cigar smoke and decaying seaweed. In the centre of the parking lot stood a single street lamp that illuminated a golden circle of light onto the pavement below. At that moment it felt as though we were the audience of a theatre performance that had yet to begin, and so, as we sat there silently sipping our drinks, we stared at the stage with sustained expectation.

'God, I love this place,' came a voice to my right. 'Been coming here for thirty years.'

'I can see why,' I said, with complete sincerity.

I imagined myself sitting there thirty years into the future, no longer a simple guest, but an ancient formation of the unchanging motel landscape. 'I've been around the world several times,' says the unnamed narrator in the film *Sans Soleil*, 'and now only banality still interests me.' After thirty years of returning to Cape Cod, it was here that these men spent their vacation – this was the epicentre of their idealized world. In their presence, any discomfort I had found in the silence soon melted away. It was late in the holiday season and the motel was almost empty. Or, perhaps, it was always this way. I looked down to find another can of beer in my hand, despite the first one being almost full. An impromptu gathering of moths and flying insects danced in a spectral mass around the dazzling bulb of the street lamp.

I remembered the Austrian novelist Joseph Roth, who wrote about living in various European hotels just before the Second World War. 'I am a hotel citizen, a hotel-patriot,' he wrote in 1929. 'And as other men may be happy to be reunited with their pictures, their china, the silver, their children and their books, so I rejoice in the cheap wallpaper, the spotless ewer and basin, the gleaming hot and cold taps, and that wisest of books: the phone book.' Roth didn't name the hotel in question, but the translator of *The Hotel Years* said it was probably a 'composite or a dream', which, at that moment, resonated perfectly.

Hotels and motels offer the illusion of home, while also preserving the feeling of homelessness. It might be said that this is the 'motel promise' of supermodernity: homelessness even when we are still at home. The French anthropologist Marc Augé called such transitional spaces – motels, airports, gas stations, supermarkets and so on – 'non-places'. They are spaces for passage and consumption, destinations – not in themselves – but rather spaces that we pass through in transit to some place else;

spaces devoid of personal history or collective memory. In these spaces we adopt the anonymous non-identity of 'traveller'. We become strangers in a strangely familiar world. Geoff Dyer writes that the hotel lobby is the, '…passage from place to non-place'. That through the ritual of checking in and handing over your identity, by, '…becoming a temporary resident of this non-place you become a non-person… In the confines of the hotel you are no longer Mr. or Ms. Whoever, you are simply the occupant of a room. You have no history.'

Perhaps it is the spatial and temporal qualities of hotel and motel rooms that lend themselves as conduits for the two primary transitional moments of life: sex and death. Chet Baker, John Belushi, Oscar Wilde, Michael Hutchence, Janis Joplin, Coco Chanel, Walter Benjamin, Joseph Roth and countless others all checked into hotel rooms, only to check out of life.

The next morning we found ourselves in a charming roadside diner. The place was a bustling cacophony of ceramic dishes and bellowing conversation. I remembered telling S. only the night before that I would absolutely not eat again for a week. And yet, with astonishment and alarm, I heard myself ordering a double stack of pancakes. S. sat across the table, expressionless, wearing a pair of oversized prescription sunglasses that she had found under the front seat of the Buick, quite unconcerned by my distress.

'Seriously, can you take them off?' I said. 'You're creeping everyone out.'

The waitress returned with my pancakes and silently filled our cups with tepid, watery coffee. She was perhaps in her late fifties, had tangled blonde hair and a faded tattoo etched across her forearm that I think may have said *saved*.

'What's the name of this town?' I asked the waitress. I already knew the answer but I wanted to hear her voice, and when it came it was as tender and vernal as I had hoped.

S. snatched the plate of pancakes and dragged it across the table in front of her.

'Did you know,' she mumbled, through a mouthful of food, 'that in the past it was common for cartographers to put fictional towns into their maps?'

'What, as a practical joke?'

'Not at all. They were as a kind of secret watermark to prevent competitors from stealing their designs. They called them "paper towns". They weren't always towns, though, sometimes they were streets or mountains or some other non-existent landmark.'

'Interesting.'

'I know. But get this: in the 1930s two cartographers made an anagram from both their names and invented a town they called Agloe. They inserted this fictional place into their map of New York State, buried among other real towns. Then, several years after the map went on sale, Agloe was spotted on a map produced by a competitor company.'

'So they got caught out,' I said, reclaiming my breakfast.

'Well, actually things got strange when this competitor company argued in court that, in fact, Agloe existed, and they could prove it. You see, on the actual site of Agloe was the Agloe General Store. And so they were right, the Agloe General Store legitimized Agloe as a real place.'

'You're saying someone built a store and named it after the unknowingly fictional town name on the map?' I asked.

'Correct.'

'Huh,' I said, unbuttoning my pants to relieve the anticipated pressure. 'It's like the act of naming had ruptured some thin membrane that separates the imaginary from reality.'

'Exactly,' said S. 'And Agloe held its place in the real world even after the general store went out of business. It continued to exist on maps into the 1990s. Until recently you could even look it up on Google Maps. I saw it a few times, but then one day it disappeared even from there.'

'So basically,' I said, 'the fictional town became a real town, and then it became a fictional town again.'

'It's as if maps are not representations of the world, but objects for its creation. We think that the stream of reality to representation flows just one way, but maybe, on rare occasions, the tide turns and the stream flows back upon itself.'

'It's like maps are just illusions of reality.'

'Right,' said S. 'The three-dimensional world magically compressed into two dimensional form.'

We were back in the car and driving south. Through the side window I watched the passing stream of gas stations, seedy motels and roadside diners, signs advertising advance loans, used-car dealerships and half-built apartment blocks. They lined the road, blooming their messages in neon lights like the flowers of noxious weeds that grow among the ruins of urban decay.

It was easy to see, even after so many years, why Hopper had been drawn to Cape Cod. He saw a version of America invisible to everyone else, but now it was impossible to see it without seeing Hopper. 'The look of an asphalt road as it lies in the broiling sun at noon,' wrote Hopper, 'cars and locomotives lying in God-forsaken railway yards, the steaming summer rain that can fill us with such hopeless boredom, the bland concrete walls and steel construction of modern industry, mid-summer streets with the acrid green of closecut lawns, the dusty Fords and gilded movies – all the sweltering, tawdry life of the American small town ... the sad desolation of our suburban landscape.'

What if, like Roth's cherished hotel, Hopper's *Gas* is not one gas station, but rather a composite of gas stations? Or a dream? Hopper's defining character is, after all, that of placelessness. It seemed entirely appropriate, even righteous, that Hopper's gas station should not exist beyond the limits of the canvas.

S. abruptly swerved into a bustling red and white Mobile gas station. From the outside, the gleaming cement and acrylic structure appeared futuristic and otherworldly.

'I don't think this is it,' I announced in my best ironic voice.

'The car needs gas. And I need caffeine.'

We pulled up next to an oversized campervan from which bicycles, fishing rods and various neon-coloured floatation devices clung like decorations to a Christmas tree. While S. filled the tank, I slipped on my sneakers and got out. I walked around the back of the campervan, which was masked by a collage of stickers announcing various messages about supporting troops and chastizing Obama. I strolled through the climate-controlled interior of the gas station, past aisles of chocolate bars, engine oil and plastic flags, to a stout ice-cream freezer in the back.

Above the freezer, attached to the wall, was a road map of Massachusetts. It had been opened and closed enough times before being attached to the wall for faded brown lines to cut a worn grid across its surface, and in places small holes had emerged through the topography. At the location I assumed to be the gas station, a large red pin had been pushed into the map, crucifying it to the plaster wall. In this gesture I found a kind of obtuse violence.

I paid for the gas, two coffees, a packet of cheese crisps, and at the last moment picked up a modern edition map of New England. When I returned to the car, S. was scanning through the radio stations. I was relieved to see she hadn't done a *Vanishing* on me.

'Where do you want to go now?' she asked, squinting into the afternoon sun.

'Let's hit the beach one more time and then head back.'

'But what about Hopper's gas station?'

'Whatever,' I said. 'I doubt it ever existed. Or if it did, it no longer does. Or if it does, it's not worth the effort. Either way, I no longer care.'

I opened the map of New England. It was shiny and virginal, brimming with road-trip potential.

'To me the important thing is the sense of going on. You know how beautiful things are when you're travelling,' I said, sipping my coffee.

'That's rather whimsical,' said S.

'Actually, I was quoting Hopper.'

Looking at the map, I read out various small-town names one after the other.

'There's a Mistake Island in Maine,' I said. 'Let's go there.'

'That *must* be a paper town.' She laughed, coaxing the deep rumble of the engine to life.

As we drove home I thought about Hopper's gas station, wherever it may be, and the future pilgrims that will visit the site, which, given enough time, will be marked with a memorial plaque. 'Here once stood the gas station depicted in Edward Hopper's iconic painting *Gas*.' They will take photographs of the site, now nothing more than a bare patch of sandy soil concealed by weeds and shrubs. They will imagine the white homely structure and its short, balding station attendant. And perhaps, for just a moment, they will feel the emanating presence of a space charged with the memory of place.

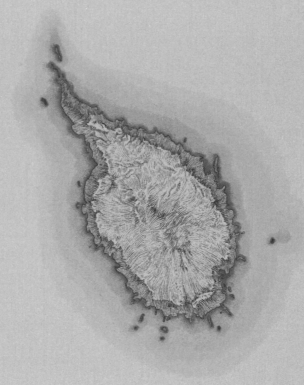

Little Hope Island

Little Hope Island, Nova Scotia, Canada

ONE COULD BE mistaken for thinking Little Hope is the younger sibling of another island, perhaps a larger version of itself called Hope, or even Big Hope. But that is not the case. What is surprising is that a tiny, unassuming island, little more than a mound of stones which one can traverse from shore to shore in under a minute, could harbour such a malevolent reputation as ship-wrecker. In 1866, the government of Nova Scotia had decidedly had enough and the island was furnished with a lighthouse, a tiny house for its keeper and a storage shed. The three micro-structures crowded the entire surface area of the island, giving it a bizarre, fairy-tale appearance. Shortly after its completion, an 1873 article in the *Canadian Illustrated News* commented, '… it can easily be imagined how some Saxby tidal wave could effectively wipe out from the face of this creation this lonely islet with its lighthouse, lighthouse keeper, his wife and all,' suggesting later that, '…the keeper of the lighthouse in such a lonely position should be well remunerated'.

Lighthouse keeper; perhaps no two other words can effectively conjure such an image of romantic melancholy. We see a sandstone cliff or a windswept island and on it a solitary white cylinder braves an unrelenting battery of waves. Its silver beam slices through the dark of night, like a blade cutting through a black velvet curtain. Inside sits the keeper. The warm glow of a candle flame dances shadows across his bearded face. He is surrounded by simple objects: a pile of worn books, a half-empty whisky bottle. In his thick, weathered hand he nurses a wooden pipe, perhaps one of many crafted over countless nights from the driftwood that washes ashore after winter storms. On other nights, by the light of a lantern, he may dabble in poetry, although no one will ever see it.

The popular perception of lighthouse keepers as enigmatic and sagacious hermits dates back to Saint Venerius, known also as Venerius the Hermit. Around the year AD 600, Venerius left his Italian monastery to seek a life of greater austerity on the remote Isle of Tino, earning him the prodigious title of Patron Saint of Lighthouse Keepers. Religious hermits like Venerius, including anchorites and anchoresses, traditionally sought a solitary existence in stone cells or hermitages attached to churches or monasteries. For a period during the 17th century, it was popular among wealthy British aristocracy to ornament one's garden with a hermit. This hermit resided in a small hut or shelter, often dressing in druid fashion for the voyeuristic pleasure of visitors and guests. More than a whimsical garden feature, they represented the most celebrated of Victorian emotions – that of melancholy. Those persons exhibiting a state of contemplation and a solemn disposition were valued as noble among the bourgeoisie and their hermits were asked to embody this. In return, the hermit would receive food, housing and occasionally a small monthly allowance. Their arcane lifestyle and quasi-religious affiliation gave them a mystical aura, for which they were often sought out for spiritual advice. As lighthouses became more common along coastlines, they also grew in popularity with hermits, offering them both social reclusion and intimacy with nature.

For nearly a hundred years, eleven solitary men called Little Hope Island home. Perhaps the most remarkable is Alan Langille, who from 1927 to 1945 served as lighthouse keeper. At first he was joined by his family, but after four years of solitary island life they abandoned him for civilization. Langille,

Saint Venerius the Hermit, no. 21 from *Trophaeum Vitae Solitariae* (*Lives of the Hermits*). Image courtesy of fine arts museum of San Francisco.

however, was no quitter. While the world raged around him, Little Hope stood as an island outside of time. Events passed as if on a distant planet: Lindbergh flies solo across the Atlantic, penicillin is discovered, the stock market crashes, Pluto is discovered, scientists split the atom, prohibition ends, the cheeseburger is created, Alcoholics Anonymous is founded, Germany invades Poland, Stone Age cave paintings are found in France, the Japanese attack Pearl Harbor, D-day, Germany surrenders, America drops atomic bombs on Hiroshima and Nagasaki, the first computer is built, and then, after eighteen years, Alan Langille returned to a world quite unlike the one he'd left.

In 1945 Little Hope's lighthouse was automated, bringing an end to nearly a hundred years of lighthouse keepers. Today, lighthouses around the world, and their human keepers, are an endangered species. Each year, advances in mapping and navigation bring about the demise of these monuments to the old world. Decades of disuse saw Little Hope's lighthouse fall into disrepair and then ruin. After a powerful winter storm in December 2003, Nova Scotia fishermen looked out over the ocean at an uninterrupted skyline, and it was not what they saw that saddened them, but what they didn't see: Little Hope's lighthouse had finally been washed from existence.

Little Hope Island, photographed in 1947.
Image courtesy of Ken Burrows.

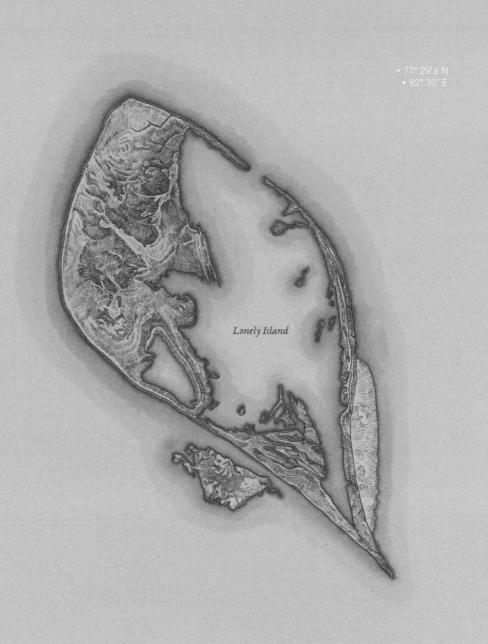

• 77° 29'a N
• 82° 30' E

Lonely Island

Lonely Island, Kara Sea, Russia

'AN ISLAND,' WRITES D. Graham Burnett in his essay *On the Monstrosity of Islands*, 'is a bit of earth that has broken faith with the terrestrial world. This quite naturally gives rise to concern about the reliability and good will of these landforms, which have so clearly turned their back on geographical solidarity. Creeping anxiety along these lines likely accounts in some measure for the prominence of islands in the robust literatures of betrayal, solitude, madness and despair.'

At the centre of the Kara Sea, hundreds of miles above the Arctic Circle, sits an island in permanent deep freeze. For most of the year, this tiny piece of frozen rock lies encased in ice and snow, with heaving ice packs enclosing the island in all directions, turning sea and island into a single rigid landmass. Bitter Arctic winds tear across its surface, sculpting a frozen, hostile landscape. During the brief summer, when the ice releases its furious grip, hungry polar bears can be seen scavenging for a meal.

A 1967 stamp celebrating Soviet science fiction.

In 1878 when the Norwegian explorer Edvard Holm Johannesen discovered this solitary formation of rock, he named it *Ensomheden*: Lonely Island. It wasn't seen again until 1915 by the Norwegian ship *Eklips*, which had been given the impossible task of searching for the missing Rusanov expedition that had embarked two years earlier on a mission to navigate the elusive Northern Sea Route – only to disappear in the Kara Sea without a trace. In the early 1920s, two Soviet expeditions attempted to find Lonely Island. However, when they reached its location, it was nowhere to be seen. In the preceding years, its whereabouts remained a mystery, with rumours spreading that it was nothing more than a phantom landmass.

It wasn't until 1933 that Otto Schmidt, aboard the *Chelyuskin*, discovered the illusory island by chance, while also attempting to be the first to navigate the Northern Sea Route – this time successfully. It was found fifty miles north-west of where Johannesen had originally mapped it in 1878 and it was named again, in Russian, *Uyedineniya*: Solitude Island. The Soviets wouldn't let it slip away this time. The following year they constructed a polar research station and selected a group of lucky scientists and auxiliary staff to inhabit the base: a radio technician and operator, a doctor, a carpenter, several meteorologists, a hydrologist, two mechanics, an aerological technician, one cook and a servant.

Back in the motherland, the golden age of Soviet literature was just beginning to flourish. Despite state censorship, writers were prolific and experimental; engaged with science, exploration, space, philosophy, ethics, utopian and dystopian concepts, they used allegories of distant planets, parallel worlds and imaginary futures to quietly subvert and satirize utopian socialist ideals. Islands of the future existed not in oceans but in space. Arkady and Boris Strugatsky's 1969 novel *The Inhabited Island* follows the young, and somewhat naive, interstellar explorer Maxim Kammerer who becomes stranded on the unknown planet of Saraksh. He thinks of himself as a Robinson Crusoe, shipwrecked on an island populated by primitive but friendly natives. It turns out to be less alluring, when his tropical island is in fact a totalitarian state, ruled by an anonymous oligarchy called the Unknown Fathers. The filthy city is inhabited by a deprived and miserable population, brainwashed into loyalty to the oppressive government by means of secret mind-control broadcasts. It's not difficult to see the underlying satire that radiates from every line of the brothers Strugatsky's book.

The few stories of Lonely Island are far bleaker than any science fiction novel. During the depths of one particularly long winter, the bar supply on the island had run disturbingly low, until a time came when not a single drop of alcohol was to be found within hundreds of miles. In a deranged state of desperation, several meteorologists, tormented by the prospect of months of potential sobriety, upended storage boxes and forgotten supplies in search of any intoxicating liquids. To their relief, they at last uncovered a wooden barrel. Neglected for years, it contained a strong-smelling concoction and, with the hearty enthusiasm of parched, lost wanderers emerging from the African desert, they unhesitatingly downed the unsavoury brew. A joyful eruption of singing and dancing drifted late into the Arctic night. However, by morning the men were dead. Closer examination of a faded label suggested their killer to be none other than methanol, likely once used as antifreeze.

One evening in September 1942, Lonely Island was bombed by a Nazi U-boat, one of the last actions of Operation Wunderland. The submarine was simply passing through the neighbourhood when the commander decided to bomb the seven hapless scientists asleep in their research station. Rudely awoken by the unfolding havoc, they leapt from their beds in their pyjamas and scrambled into the snow to escape the bombardment. Satisfied by the level of destruction, the U-boat continued on its way back to base. The shelling destroyed four radio stations, the men's sleeping quarters and the pigsty. The casualties numbered two pigs and the garrison.

No humans live on Lonely Island, at least not any more. Temperatures barely rise above zero even during the summer, preserving the weather station like a Siberian woolly mammoth. Never-expiring cans of peaches and ham wait patiently on shelves. The walls inside the mess hall are painted California blue and decorated with tropical palm trees. The stern and serious face of Lenin, posed in that side profile for which he is best recognized, stares out from a poster that hangs next to a timber door labelled 'Bar'. Russian scientists occasionally fly there in prehistoric helicopters to conduct weather experiments. Like tourists to an archaic museum, they wander the bleak diorama, gazing in wonder at the preserved artifacts of their Soviet ancestors; taking photos, rummaging through piles of discarded objects, searching for souvenirs as evidence of their journey into the past.

If Lonely Island were not real, it would make a fitting work of science fiction. Or then again, as Aldous Huxley once remarked, 'Maybe this world is another planet's Hell.'

World's End

World's End, London, England

T HE WORLD OF King James II must have seemed very small indeed, for the short, leisurely trips that he took along King's Road to the outskirts of 17th-century London appeared to him as a journey to the very end of the world, for that was the name he gave it. The name stuck through the following centuries as outer London grew closer, fields disappeared beneath Victorian brick terraces, villas and workers' cottages until, in the late 1960s, it became the destitute end of Chelsea, home to both hippies and social dropouts. It was during this time that Victorian brick houses were torn down across London to make space for the modern symbol of urban poverty: high-rise social housing. In 1963 a scheme was conceived by Chelsea Borough Council to build the World's End Estate. The new high-rise social housing project was just one of many sprouting up in London throughout the 1960s and 70s in a desperate attempt to fix the city's enormous post-war housing shortage.

The architect's idealistic ambition to provide an, '…outer suburban dream for those enjoying the good life' was at odds with the public's dim view of such social housing projects. This was undoubtedly compounded by the brutalist architectural trend spreading not just across London, but around the globe at the time. When complet-ed in 1975, the seven blocks of the World's End Estate appeared more like a medieval fortified prison than what one might imagine the 'outer suburban dream' to look like. However, this was no coincidence. Architectural theories of 'defensible space' at the time promoted design that responded to the onslaught of so-called 'anti-social behaviour' infecting urban, high-density housing. The World's End Estate was just one of many new brutalist projects shooting up across the London skyline, urban fortresses made from monolithic slabs of rough utilitarian materials such as glass, brick and concrete. Originating from the French *béton brut,* meaning 'raw concrete', the term 'brutalism' was unleashed into the popular vernacular by the British architectural critic Reyner Banham to identify the bold, new architectural trend. Promoted by a generation of young, restless architects, the style aimed to shake the foundations of a stale British bourgeois society. However, its uncanny resemblance to Nazi fortification bunkers mixed with the utopian ideology of the socialist east was not lost on the conservative British public, who loathed the brutalist aesthetic. The style has seen renewed affection among younger generations, too young to be afflicted by the trauma of the Second World War and the Soviet threat.

Across London, numerous examples of brutalist architecture can still be found: Balfron Tower, Alexandra Road Estate,

Robin Hood Gardens and Barbican Estate, to name just a few. The Brunel University Lecture Centre had its dystopian identity reinforced when it featured in Stanley Kubrick's film *A Clockwork Orange*. Perhaps the most infamous example is the Trellick Tower, aka 'The Tower of Terror' or 'Colditz in the Sky'. Finished in 1972, it was designed by the fantastically named Hungarian architect Ernö Goldfinger, whose name (much to the humourless architect's irritation) was appropriated by Ian Fleming as an evil James Bond villain. Stories of random stabbings, rapes in the elevators, heroin addicts attacking children and suicides featured regularly in newspapers. It was even rumoured that Goldfinger, so distraught by the monstrous creature to which he had given life, threw himself from the building's roof. (In actuality, he simply moved out.)

The World's End Estate stands apart from many of its brutalist siblings in that its prefab concrete exterior is clad in red brick – an aesthetic attempt to appease which others bitterly saw as a mockery of the red-brick Victorian houses that it replaced. While the estate experienced little of the destructive mayhem of Trellick Tower, it was still trapped in the overall dismal view of brutalist, urban, high-rise housing.

In 1975, when London author J.G. Ballard released his novel *High-Rise*, a fictional account of a London residential high-rise slowly transforming into a dystopian nightmare, the popular imagination had been thoroughly primed. The book traces the building's social collapse as its 2,000 upper/middle-class residents descend from trivial bickering into bloody warfare, tribal savagery and cannibalism to self-destruction. Ballard's inspiration for the book was to be found all around him. Besides the obvious brutalist models in London, a series of disturbing experiments in urban living and population density were taking place. During the 1960s, ethologist John Calhoun built a series of experimental 'mouse cities' at the National Institute of Mental Health in Poolesville, Maryland. He called them 'Universes'. Perhaps the most infamous was Universe 25, a square tank measuring 2.5 metres square surrounded by high walls from which the mice couldn't escape. There were 256 nesting boxes, each capable of housing fifteen mice. Everything was provided – an abundance of fresh water, food and nesting materials. It was a mouse utopia. On the first day, four pairs of mice were introduced, and after familiarizing themselves with their new home, they started to reproduce. The population exploded, doubling every fifty-five days. During the brief golden age of Universe 25, the city's residents flourished in harmonious co-existence. But as the population peaked and space became increasingly scarce, Calhoun observed disturbing behaviour. Baby mice were neglected. Males became aggressive and hyper-sexual. Living mice cannibalized the dead.

Apart from a group of males Calhoun called 'The Beautiful Ones', who spent their days secluded from the world, enveloped in the egocentric pleasures of eating, sleeping and grooming, disinterested both in sex and violence, Universe 25 plummeted from utopia to dystopia. On day 560, the population peaked at 2,200 mice. After this

there were few pregnancies and no surviving young. Universe 25 rapidly descended into extinction. It requires only a small imaginative leap to draw parallels between Universe 25 and urban habitation. Calhoun himself encouraged the associations by referring to the mouse dwellings as 'tower blocks' and 'walk-up apartments'. The 1960s was a time when fear of overpopulation leading to food shortage, global chaos and human extinction was imminent in the popular imagination.

While we may indeed be in the midst of anthropogenic extinction, for which, many have argued, the evidence is all around, London's brutalist social housing has seen an unlikely concrete renaissance. Trellick Tower was declared by one new paper as 'terrifying but now fashionable' and was even awarded a Grade II (important buildings of more than special interest) listing in 1998. 'This was an environment built, not for man, but for man's absence,' J.G. Ballard writes in *High-Rise*. Perhaps the same could be said about the world we live in.

Calhoun inside one of his mouse utopias in 1970.
Image by Yoichi R. Okamoto, White House photographer.

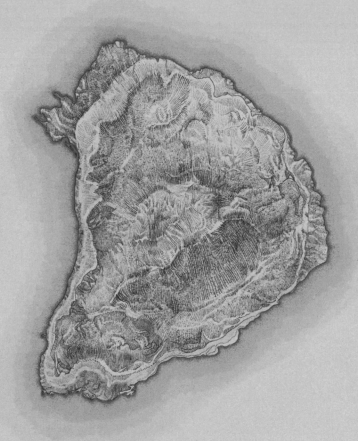

Isle of the Dead

• 43°08 57 S
  • 147°52 03 E

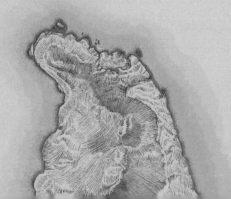

Isle of the Dead, Tasmania, Australia

Isle of the Dead, 3rd version, Arnold Böcklin (1883).
Alte Nationalgalerie, Berlin.

F OR SIX YEARS, between 1880 and 1886, the Swiss artist Arnold Böcklin painted a series of five images in his Florence studio, each depicting the same nightmarish island. White stone cliffs rise vertically into a dark, storm-laden sky. The island has the form of a horseshoe, the bay opening towards the viewer, revealing a series of burial chambers cut deep into the rock face. From the heart of the island grows a cluster of impossibly tall cypress trees, their dark foliage forming a single, ominous mass that fills the centre of the canvas. A small wooden boat glides across calm water towards the bay, rowed by a man whose face we cannot see. His passenger is a figure shrouded in white cloth, standing over a coffin. The island is illuminated from the dark sea by a fading sun.

Each of the five paintings portrays the same island, yet each is slightly different. It is as if Böcklin was haunted by a reccurring dream – each painting an attempt to pin down exact details that evaded his waking mind – and by recreating the same scene, over and over, he could, somehow, be released from its spell. He gave all five paintings the same title: *Isle of the Dead*.

Unbeknown to Böcklin, on the other side of the world was the island that haunted his dreams. The sheer strangeness of this fact is compounded by the nightmarish circumstances by which the real Isle of the Dead had been born into existence.

Between 1788 and 1868, serious overcrowding in London's prisons inspired officials to transport approximately 162,000 criminals to various penal colonies around the newly formed country of Australia. One could expect to be deported for such offences as, 'stealing a fish from a pond or lake', 'stealing roots, trees or plants', 'clandestine marriage' or even, mysteriously, for, 'impersonating an Egyptian'. One could even be sent to Australia for simply being homeless. Penal colonies were renowned for their harsh cruelty, but none more so than Port Arthur. Converted from a timber station to a prison in 1830, its isolated location on Van Diemen's Land – now Tasmania – was perfect for undesirable criminals who needed further punishment. Port Arthur's penal system adopted an early version of 'Separate Prison Typology', outlined by the British philosopher and social theorist Jeremy Bentham. The 'Separate Prison System' signalled a shift from standard punishment – such as public floggings – to a more refined practice of psychological punishment.

'The question,' asked Bentham, 'is not can they reason, nor can they talk – but can they suffer?' Bentham insisted that physical punishment only served to harden the prisoner, while psychological punishment could break them down from the inside.

Those unfortunate enough to arrive on the shores of Port Arthur were treated to an entire year in solitary confinement in Separation Prison. Bentham's prescription for prison silence was implemented with extreme rigour. Each man was locked in a single cell built from thick, stone walls

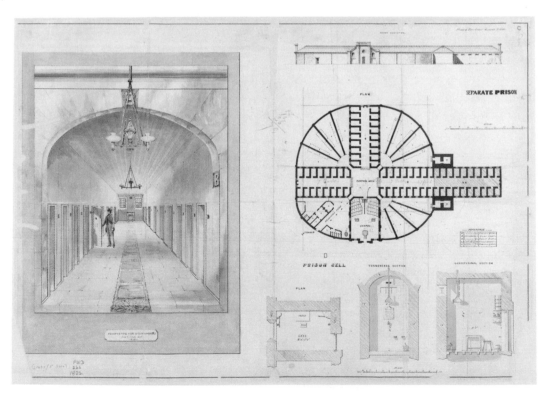

Separate Prison architectural plans.
Image courtesy of the Tasmanian Archive and Heritage Office.

– impenetrable to sound. Prisoners were forbidden to speak at all times. Guards patrolled in felt slippers and communicated to each other in sign language. For a single hour each day the prisoner was allowed, alone and hooded, into the courtyard. Once a week they were ushered, again hooded, into a specially designed chapel with private walled-off pews. So many prisoners were psychologically disturbed by the experience that a mental asylum was built next to the prison. Physical violence was replaced with psychological terror. Böcklin had made a comparative transition in his *Isle of the Dead* paintings. Unlike other works of gruesome horror such as Artemisia Gentileschi's 1614 painting *Judith Slaying Holofernes*, or Goya's grisly masterpiece *Saturn Devouring His Son* from 1819 – in which a monstrous creature tears the limbs from a child's body with the ferocious vigour that one may employ to eat a particularly tough baguette sandwich – the fear induced by Böcklin's *Isle of the Dead* is a subtle, Hitchcockian fear; the haunting kind that lurks deep in the recesses of your mind only to re-emerge during the perils of sleep. The painting is, '…so silent', Böcklin himself noted, 'that you would get a fright if there was a knock at the door'.

Astonishingly, Separation Prison earned a name for itself as a pioneering institution in the development of a new and enlightened system of prisoner conditioning and penal reform. With the aid of mere darkness, silence and loneliness, the punishment of the silent system was to turn the mind against itself, to facilitate an environment in which the horrors of night were both internal and eternal – a place where nightmares were free to ravage the mind into irreversible insanity.

Those who emerged after a year in Separation Prison were as traumatized and deranged as one might expect. Apart from murders and drownings, a great number died from diseases such as dysentery and scurvy. Some attempted to escape, others murdered – an offence punishable by death – as a means to escape the desolation of prison life. Bodies of the dead were rowed one mile across the bay to the Isle of the Dead where they were dumped into graves around the island, marked with nothing more than a mound of dirt.

The only resident on the Isle of the Dead was the gravedigger, who lived in a small wooden hut. The first gravedigger was a quiet Irish prisoner named Barron who died after twenty years of living alone on the island. After his body was promptly moved from wooden hut to dirt hole, he was replaced with another prisoner named Mark Jeffrey, who found comfort in the digging of his own grave, which he lovingly tended on a daily basis. Unfortunately for Jeffrey, he would never get to enjoy his cherished grave. His stay on the island ended abruptly when, one morning, guards at Port Arthur were called to the island by a signal fire.

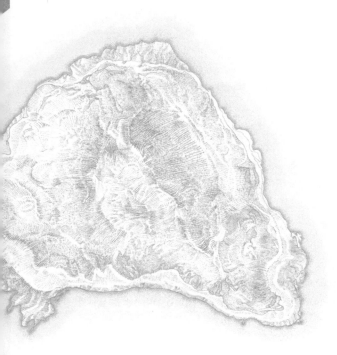

After arriving, they found Jeffrey in a state of panic. He recalled that during the night his hut had been violently shaken by an invisible force, after which he received a visit from 'His Satanic Majesty'. Jeffrey refused to stay another night on the island.

Writer George Gruncell visited the prison several times during the 1870s, later recalling in his diary a funeral he witnessed. He describes a coffin being carried from the church to a small wooden boat manned by a crew dressed in white cloth. 'A start [was] made across the bay to Dead Island. The water was very calm and the sinking sun shed a parting ray of light upon the Isle of the Dead, and threw it out in bold and bright relief against the darker background of distant hills beyond… Landing upon a rocky ledge a procession was formed which was conducted by the gravedigger until we reached the spot where the last of the convict inhabitants was to be interred.'

Atlas
of
Melancholy

Expulsion from the Garden of Eden, Thomas Cole (1828).
Museum of Fine Arts, Boston.

'Nobility is only in the negation of existence, in a smile that surveys annihilated landscapes.'
E.M. CIORAN, *A Short History of Decay*

It was some years ago, on a crisp autumn afternoon, that I found myself in Boston's Museum of Fine Arts. It was Sunday and the museum was swollen to maximum capacity. It must have been free entry for pensioners because, much like the art, everyone in the museum appeared archaic and fragile. The young and able, I suddenly realized, must be at the *contemporary* art museum across town. Elderly bodies propped vertical with various devices formed a slow-shifting, unnavigable river that meandered painfully between rooms. The air was thick with the odour of musk and stale sweat and, as Didion put it, '…a silence we have come to expect and want from the past'. Any possibility for a meaningful art-having experience seemed increasingly unlikely.

Golden sunlight cascaded down in dusty columns over grey stone walls, on which oil paintings of ancient myths hung, creating an atmosphere more akin to a European cathedral than an art museum. There is an unspoken understanding – unique to both museums and places of religious worship – that an impetuous laugh or unrestrained expression of enthusiasm is sinful and will invite the disapproving glare of fellow patrons and guards alike, who, with a mixture of suspicion and bore-dom, will continue to study you as punishment for upsetting the sacred ambience. One may have thought that the radical, post-Enlightenment separation of art from religion would also require some radical re-evaluation of one's social experience of art, but it isn't so. When I saw Duchamp's *Fountain* in the Tate Modern some years back, I was surprised to find myself, along with everyone else, silently brooding over the porcelain urinal as if it were an ancient religious artifact. We were basking in the auratic glow shed by this mystical object like a cluster of hobos warming themselves by an oil-drum fire. It would appear we are so religiously institutionalized that we voluntarily act with the same sullen and reflective behaviour in museums as we do in churches, as if the conditions for both artistic and religious enlightenment require the same austere containment of human emotion.

This half-conceived thought was broken by the sound of violent weeping coming from an adjacent room. I waded through the wrinkled flesh to search for what I hoped would be someone overwhelmed by a profound experience of art. Before a wall-size depiction of Napoleon straddling a white horse, a stout, lumpy man in woollen slacks was doubled over, furiously coughing out his lungs into a pale yellow handkerchief. Disappointed and weary, I searched for an unoccupied bench, of which there seemed to be an unacceptable shortage. Instead, I found myself queuing behind a cluster of elderly women sporting audio guides. They were huddled around a large oil canvas bathed in meticulously calibrated light. Like a group of mourners at a funeral, each stepped forward one at a time to pay their respects and admire the craftsmanship of the undertaker at bringing the dead back to life.

The women moved on and I approached the painting. *Expulsion from the Garden of Eden, Thomas Cole, 1828.* On the right-hand side of the painting, Eden is depicted in all its customary paradisiacal splendour: swans bathe among lush green forests and deer frolic under glorious morning light. By contrast, the left-hand side of the painting, the un-Eden, is a furious shit-storm. Evidence of death, violence and destruction litter the landscape. In the distance, an erupting volcano spews fire and ash into a forbidding sky. Among the debris of a storm-ravaged forest, a snarling wolf fends off a hungry vulture from the corpse of a deer. The world of un-Eden is almost monochromatic, as if all colour, along with life itself, has drained from the canvas. And then, there, in the bottom left-hand corner, are Adam and Eve: two tiny, butt-naked figures edging out into a decaying landscape. Eve strides ahead. Clearly eager to gain distance from God's wrath, her head hangs in a gesture that suggests both guilt and shame. She grasps Adam by the hand who, a few steps in tow, stares back at the blast of divine light, bewildered and aggrieved and slapping his forehead as if to say, 'Seriously, what the fuck?' Like an intoxicated party-goer, he feels the punishment of eternal eviction from Club Eden is surely unjust. The world into which they are cast, the world beyond Eden, is more than wild and untamed: it's unmistakably apocalyptic. It's as if God expelled our ancestors into a distant future in which humans already lived, exhausted all natural resources, pumped the atmosphere with carbonic gases and retired into extinction – and now all that remains are the final fits and seizures of a planet writhing on its death bed. So this, I thought to myself, is how we humans emerged. Two sad people stepping out into an even sadder world.

Two sad people.

To my immense disappointment, they did not have the painting as a postcard in the gift store. 'No sir,' said a cashier, not even looking up from his computer, 'we do not have it as a fridge magnet, coffee mug or snow globe either.' During the car ride out of the city, I was struck by a further revelation as to why we humans, who live in such prosperous times, should also be inflicted with a strange melancholy. We did not stride triumphantly out of Eden – hot off the press, ready to invigorate a new and glorious world. Instead, we slunk out whimpering, intoxicated with a nostalgia of such potency as to permanently alter the genetic makeup of all posterity.

Robert Burton was already onto this idea in the early 17th century when he wrote *The Anatomy of Melancholy*. 'This noble creature is fallen from that he was … to become one of the most miserable creatures of the world. How much altered from that

he was; before blessed and happy, now miserable and accursed…
subject to death and all manner of infirmities, all kind of
calamities.' It was in my first year of art school that I came across
a copy of *Anatomy* in a second-hand bookstore. The hulking
mass of paper dominated all other books on the shelf, which
groaned audibly when I relieved it of its burden. The cover
featured a painting of a human skull and hourglass: archetypal
symbols of death and time, which when placed together suggest ephemeral mortality – the essence of melancholy. While I
had never heard of Robert Burton, I was charmed by the
quasi-scientific title, the worn and malformed spine, and – with
no actual intention of reading the book – was further seduced
by the prospect of its masterly presence on my bookshelf next to
the unread Deleuze, Foucault, Spinoza and Lacan.

After returning home I instead found the book more effi-
cacious when located next to my bed. On the rare occasions a
female entered my room, the book – by its sheer physical mass
– generated a kind of gravitational pull, drawing all matter and
life towards it, and thus, to my bed. Sometimes, I would heave
the book open and read from a random page: 'He that increaseth
wisdom, increaseth sorrow.' 'Melancholy can be overcome
only by melancholy.' 'If you like not my writing, go read
something else.' I cannot say for certain that Burton's ancient
wisdom played any useful role in getting me laid, but the mere
presence of *Anatomy* in my life aided in constructing the fledg-
ling – and completely naive – notion of myself as a contemporary
Romantic. Melancholy, much like voluntary poverty, an ironic
wardrobe, a postmodern haircut and benign alcoholism, was,
and possibly still is, an essential criterion for any prospective
art student.

During the intervening years, I've had time to acquaint myself with the book, which is not to say I've actually read it. First

published in 1621, *The Anatomy of Melancholy* was Burton's magnum opus, growing in later editions to some 1,400 pages. It is a tightly woven tapestry of quotes, anecdotes, observations, inventories, lists, remedies, long recitals of Latin poetry and rambling digressions that are occasionally insightful but more frequently humorous. It's perhaps because of the book's depressing subject matter that Burton approaches it with unusual playfulness. For the introduction he assumes the guise of one 'Democritus Junior' (the successor to the Laughing Philosopher of ancient Greece), stating from the outset: 'I write of melancholy, by being busy to avoid melancholy.' It's as if he's saying, *I'm doing this for my own benefit, but tag along if you want.* Frequently, Burton departs from scholarly reflection to muse over some thought that has randomly strayed into his mind, such as whether devils also shit, then promptly apologizes to the reader for this wayward thought.

As a subject, melancholy rejects categorical placement, eludes simple definition and persists defiantly throughout centuries of philosophical and scientific prodding. It is beautiful, complex and contradictory. The word literally means black bile, deriving from Greek: *melas* (black) and *chole* (bile). From the ancient Greeks until the Enlightenment it was understood that the body was made up of four humours, consisting of yellow bile and black bile, phlegm and blood. When the humours were in balance, a person remained healthy, while an imbalance was the cause of all illness and disease. Melancholy, it was believed, was the result of an excess of black bile in one's body.

In 1621, when Burton wrote *Anatomy*, the Western world was on the cusp of radical change. The Enlightenment loomed around the corner and the ideas in the book were already tenuously balanced between antiquated religious concepts and early anatomical science. Yet Burton simply wasn't satisfied with blaming Adam and Eve's mischievous fruit-snacking for the excessive black bile flowing through the veins of humankind. For the rest of the book, he embarks in a strange quest to seek out the causes of melancholy, finding blame in an almost endless list of sources that ranges from gambling to ambition, excessive studying, envy, poverty, romance, evil spirits, devils, magicians and astrology, to simply getting old. Love he declares as one of the worst culprits, dedicating an entire chapter to its torments that could easily be a book in itself. 'Love is a plague, a torture, a hell,' he writes, '…the Spanish Inquisition is not comparable to it.' To banish any remaining ambiguity, he further declares, 'Shall I say, most part of a lovers' life is full of agony, anxiety, fear and grief, complaints, sighs, suspicions, and cares…full of silence and irksome solitariness?'

Much like love, he insists food is highly problematic and best avoided. He provides helpful suggestions for those afflicted by melancholy in a kind of Robert Burton Diet (akin in its unflinching austerity to the breatharian diet, cabbage soup diet or cigarette diet), tentatively discussing and outright dismissing almost everything and anything that can be put in one's mouth. The notion that 'you are what you eat' was taken very seriously by Burton. Food didn't simply cause melancholy, it *contained* melancholy.

This implication is crucial: Burton implies that melancholy is somehow external to the human condition; an entity in its own right, an organism with agency. It is this that makes melancholy so interesting and distinct from its synonymic relatives – having the ability to transcend the human condition and inhabit the world at large. 'Kingdoms and provinces are melancholy, cities and families, all creatures, vegetable, sensible, and rational – that all sorts, sects, ages, conditions, are out of tune,' writes Burton. Melancholy would earn its edge of beauty and genius later, thanks to the Romantics and later mopy *poètes maudits* like Baudelaire, Verlaine and Lautréamont. And by the 21st century many would come to believe depression to be melancholy's contemporary equivalent, with complete disregard for the aesthetic, reflective and creative qualities that make it distinct. Susan Sontag writes that, 'Depression is melancholy minus its charms', while Alain de Botton insists that it is, '…not a disorder that needs to be cured'. 'Melancholy is a twilight state,' Victor Hugo declares in *Toilers of the Sea*, 'suffering melts into it and becomes a sombre joy. Melancholy is the pleasure of being sad.'

Melancholy is woven into the fabric of the world but is given life through the act of awareness. It needs to be induced, uncovered and wooed into existence. It's to be found concentrated in Scottish landscapes, Chet Baker's trumpet, the poetry of Wordsworth, the still-life paintings of Pieter Claesz; in the empty streets of Istanbul; in the eyes of the displaced; in the colours of late autumn; in early morning rain and in the quality of light at sunset. Yet each strain of melancholy is unique and distinct from every other, manifesting itself in innumerable ways, capable of transcending shape and form as well as time and space.

There have been a number of craftsmen throughout history who were adept conjurers of elusive melancholy. The Russian filmmaker Andrei Tarkovsky was one such individual. Every scene of every film he ever made captures landscapes drenched in nostalgia, memory and decay, that when amalgamated onto the cinema screen induces a superb melancholy in his audience. The essence of his artistic skill is concentrated in a series of Polaroids he shot between 1979 and 1984. If you can imagine transporting yourself back in time, before Polaroids were adopted by those fashionable saviours of superfluous technology, then there is something remarkable to behold. The Polaroids are compiled into a book titled *Instant Light*. The title suggests a double meaning: one referring to the magic of Polaroid photography and the other to the ephemerality of light – a distinctly *Tarkovskian* light. Light is one of the classic conduits of melancholy, specifically nostalgic melancholy, the awareness of irreconcilable estrangement from every passing moment. The content of the photographs is largely unimpressive: a glass jar of flowers on the breakfast table, a dog sitting in a misty field, an empty city street. But this misses the point. Tarkovsky urges us to look past the material and see the photographs as protests against the futility of remembrance and the absurd beauty of trying anyway. Besides the Polaroid's ability to instantly tint the world with nostalgia, what makes it melancholic is its temporality. Every photograph made on film is a unique object, one that rejects the impulse of modernity towards infinite reproduction, and thus immortality.

I have a particular fondness for the melancholy of thrift stores. The best ones – that is, the saddest ones – are dusty and cavernous mausoleums, enigmatic time capsules rich with the inimitable odour of last-stop desperation. Concealed within each object is the pain of exile, a melancholic nostalgia of that separated from its homeland. And yet these objects stubbornly march on, resisting their own cursed abandonment. In thrift stores, I am not a consumer but an anthropologist, studying each relic for traces of its surreptitious past. What of this old armchair where the sunken form of a body remains imprinted? And this woollen men's dinner jacket? If one gets close, they can inhale the rich scent of tobacco (Natural American Spirit?) fused with cheap cologne and stale sweat. In thrift stores, we are not shoppers but shamans: we possess the power to restore life to the condemned.

I find old photographs especially rich in what Roland Barthes called, '…the melancholy of photography itself'. In thrift stores, one can often find old plastic film cameras containing half or, occasionally, an entire roll of exposed film. Undeveloped film inside a camera in a thrift store suggests a reckless abandonment of the past. Perhaps death intervened before the film could be developed, or perhaps they contain memories too painful to relive in print. Whenever I happen upon such a discovery, I covertly extract the film from the lifeless body of the camera before having it developed at my local drug store. Occasionally, I hang the glossy prints on my fridge as if they were my own memories, ones from a possible future or a past that I no longer remember.

'Death is the *eidos* of photography,' writes Roland Barthes, suggesting that those people we see in old photographs have returned from the dead. But it's not only those captured in the photographs that have returned from the dead, but the paper photographs themselves. They are artifacts of a bygone world – the one of analogue photography itself. A captured image is a moment of significance, a moment deemed by the image-maker as more *momentous* than all others. A photograph is an act of defiance to memory's inadequacy and fallibility, and a photo album becomes a collection of small protests against the incoming tide of forgetting. But when lost or rejected, that memory is cast afloat into the world; its function is now nothing more than an enigmatic referent to a forgotten moment lost in time. Garry Winogrand once said that he took photographs to find out what something looks like photographed, but perhaps we take photographs to find out how something looks as a future memory.

Throughout years of thrift-store archaeology, I have accumulated several hundred old photographs, discarded fragments of past lives hidden between the pages of books, inside coat pockets or occasionally stuck in the back of abandoned photo albums. The photographs that I find among the debris of other people's lives I always steal, shamelessly slipping them in my pocket until I have reached the safety of my bedroom where, in an old shoebox, they join the sanctuary of other lost and displaced memories.

Some time ago, I came across a photograph in the back of an old library book. It was a black-and-white image of a cemetery. It looked on the surface much like any cemetery. Grey headstones sprouted from under tall dark pines. In the foreground, a short picket fence, presumably surrounding a grave. Yet curiously, from out of this grave bellowed a thick plume of white smoke. It seemed to hover in the air, as if not quite knowing where to go. In the context of the cemetery, the cloud appeared more like a spectral apparition. 'Centralia,' the image caption read poignantly, 'a dying town'. The caption did little to explain the mystery of the image, but it did succeed in piquing my curiosity. As it happened, a short time later I found myself driving with a friend from Cleveland to New York, a route that took us squarely through the American Rust Belt. I insisted on a brief stop in Centralia.

The small Pennsylvanian coal-mining town garnered international fame when in 1962 an attempt to burn the town's trash at a local landfill resulted in the fire catching to an underground coal seam. After a series of failed attempts to extinguish the fire, it spread underground like a long, unrushed fuse towards the town. Unlike tornados, hurricanes or other disasters that show up one day unannounced, the underground fire took twenty years to arrive in Centralia, like devastation delivered on the back of a turtle.

By 1984, sinkholes began spontaneously materializing around the town, steaming out columns of lethal gas. Evacuation was announced and almost all the town's 2,700 residents packed up and relocated to surrounding areas. 'This was a world where no human could live,' David DeKok wrote of Centralia in 1986, 'hotter than the planet Mercury, its atmosphere as poisonous as Saturn's. At the heart of the fire, temperatures easily exceeded 1000 degrees Fahrenheit.' In the car we played over various fantasies of the blazing inferno that awaited us; a real-world depiction of Cole's *Expulsion from the Garden of Eden*.

It was late afternoon as we approached the spot where Google Maps said the town would be. But we saw not a single sign announcing our arrival in Centralia. It was nothing like Mercury, or Saturn for that matter. Instead, we were greeted with a lush forest of trees and tangled shrubbery. Along what must have once been the main street were a number of nameless side streets that ran off at ninety-degree angles. We slowed, pulled into one, parked and got out. The thick green canopy shielded us from the June heat, making it surprisingly cool. There were no decaying ruins, not even the standard post-industrial relics of the American Rust Belt. Nor was there any suggestion of the seething inferno beneath our feet. Apart from the glistening black asphalt of the suburban streets and rusted warning signs, all traces of human existence had been neatly dissected from the landscape.

We left the car and strolled silently under oak trees, themselves horticultural vestiges, and felt like we were in a vast park through which a series of wide suburban streets had been mistakenly built. Initial disappointment immediately gave way to an all-encompassing eeriness. With some effort, it was possible to make out the lots on which houses sat some thirty years ago. The standard soundtrack of small-town America – birds, crickets, cars, lawnmowers and barking dogs – had been replaced by a weighty silence, only adding to the pervasive feeling that something beyond the material was absent from the landscape. In the negative space that is Centralia, there resides an aura of lagging consciousness and misplaced yearning, not unlike the feeling of when a person leaves a room but their presence lingers for several moments after. Centralia's status as a ghost town seemed inadequate, as even the telltale ruins of an abandoned town – the *town* part of ghost town – were absent, leaving the ghost behind. Here was a distant future where even the final remains of human history had vanished from the landscape of memory. We walked in silence to the end of the street where a carefully stacked assemblage of stained mattresses, car tyres and a single fridge lay – left as if it were a sacrificial offering made by the next town's residents to keep the subterrestrial demon at bay.

We walked further and came upon an abandoned section of PA Route 61, which I would later learn was amputated from the rest of the highway as it had become warped from the heat and too expensive to keep fixing. With nobody else around, we strode along its centre, which swept down the hill and out of sight. Its surface, which rose and fell in playful undulating waves, was decorated with bright graffiti messages. In some places the asphalt swelled up several feet and split open like a festering pimple, emitting a sharp and putrid smell that reminded me of an underground bus station. I recalled Freud, who in *Mourning and Melancholia* wrote that, '…the complex of melancholia behaves like an open wound,' suggesting that grief differs from melancholy in that while the mourner seeks closure, the melancholic embraces the prolonged suffering. If I had thought to bring a spray can, I could have imparted these words onto the road along with the thousands of other pointless messages.

By now it was almost dark and on returning to the car we noticed a woman walking in our direction. To see people walking in America outside of city centres and strip malls is always a vaguely startling experience. She wore an oversized men's business shirt that at a distance appeared floral, but as she approached the flowers crystallized into a collage of overlapping food and sweat stains. She walked with an awkward gait, perhaps down to the fact she was wearing not shoes but furry pink slippers that struck me as out of their comfort zone. Dark blue eyes glared at us from under a thick layer of asymmetrically applied makeup. A limp cigarette dangled precariously from her bottom lip. She stopped several feet ahead of us and took a long drag that caused the tip of the cigarette to blaze furiously.

'Ain't nuthin' to see here, boys.' The words came tumbling out amid a plume of grey smoke, ejected through a throat ravaged by time and carbon monoxide like the smouldering underground mines below our feet. The statement hung in the grey apparition that had materialized between the three of us – and like a fourth person who had just arrived on the scene, we stared at it until it vanished. 'Yes, ma'am,' my American friend replied while I remained sheepishly silent, staring into the void now between us. I couldn't tell if her statement had been passive-aggressive by stating the obvious to everyone, or one of genuine amazement – that she too, even after thirty years, couldn't quite believe that her town had vanished without a trace.

In silence, we drove back to Highway 80, which would take us to New York. The excited anticipation that had filled the car on the way there had now evaporated, leaving in its place a vast emptiness infused with shame and guilt at being the opportunistic voyagers we were. I thought about that woman endlessly wandering the vacant streets of a town that no longer existed. I thought about a town annihilated not by external forces, but by its own imprudent hand – that, in some abstract way, was allegorical for the current state of the world. I thought about the fire burning some 300 feet under Centralia, a fire that will continue to burn well into the Anthropocene. And I imagined, as the distant glow of New York City illuminated the horizon, what the world will be like after the fire finally dies out, if perhaps it too will be just like Centralia.

After arriving back in Boston, I returned to the Museum of Fine Arts and paid the extortionate $23 entry. (I lied about being a student for a $2 discount off the usual $25 admission fee, justifying it to myself on the grounds of being poorer now than I had been as a student.) Today, the museum was almost empty, except for a class of teenage girls who sat cross-legged in pairs, sketching abstract portraits of each other. I strode through each room with a haste I generally reserve for supermarkets, at last reaching *Expulsion*, where I immediately enacted a reflective posture.

Something now occurred to me: why had Cole intended the painting to be read from right to left? Was it to suggest that even in the mythical beginning of human history, we were already moving backwards towards annihilation? And why does the beginning of the world look so much like the end of the world? Perhaps it's the same thing: time is not linear but circular – the painting depicts the scratch on the record that causes the needle to replay the endless looping of annihilation and rebirth.

I edged as close to the painting as I could, until only an inch of museum air separated my nose from the canvas. The backward glance of Adam into the unreturnable past of Eden struck me as deeply nostalgic. Another thought occurred to me: weren't the first humans also the first refugees? Don't those gestures of despair belong to the displaced, those exiled from their homeland and cursed to forever wander the earth? Perhaps Cole had intended us to see Eden as pre-modernity, a time of childish innocence and inculpability. Perhaps Adam and

Eve are us now, melancholic and nostalgic for paradise lost –
wandering naked and lost into a world already at its end, towards
what George Williamson called the 'melancholy of living in the
afternoon of time'.

The melancholy of the Romantics was perhaps lyrical, but in
postmodernity melancholy too has evolved – it is not to be found
in ancient forests and stormy skies, but in the bleak isolation
of urban decay. I imagined that if Cole were around today and
embraced not Romantic sentimentality but a postmodern irony,
then perhaps Adam and Eve would be exiled out of Eden into
a world of endless traffic jams, of colossal shopping malls and
abandoned towns robbed even of the romance of ruins.

I left the museum and walked across the street into a park.
Brilliant afternoon light spilled through the emerald tree canopy,
forming an intricate collage of shadows that danced beneath my
feet. Unlike the museum, the park was alive; joggers and cyclists
flowed effortlessly around me as if I were a stone in a stream.
After crossing a small bridge I came to a sports field where a
circle of Lycra-clad women were exercising. I sat on a bench and
for a long time watched them perform a repetition of mysterious
athletic rituals. At this moment I felt like the nameless protago-
nist in Chris Marker's film *La Jetée* – a man who time-travels into
the past to rewrite a doomed future and instead falls in love with
both a girl and a world destined for annihilation. Like a ghost,
not from the past but from the future, he is overwhelmed by a
world now iridescent with the beauty of loss. Together, the man
and the woman wander among the dusty relics of the *Muséum
national d'Histoire naturelle* and into a Parisian park, where in the
soft afternoon light they sit on a bench. She closes her eyes while
he looks about, wearing a faint smile and he surveys annihilated
landscapes.

Darkness had drifted over so gradually as to be almost unnoticeable. In the distance, it was just possible to make out the gentle wail of a trumpet. I pulled from my bag Francis Fukuyama's *The End of History and the Last Man*, which I had bought weeks ago but had not yet opened. I flipped through the book to the last page, looking for a quick end-of-history spoiler. 'The end of history will be a very sad time,' writes Fukuyama. 'In the post-historical period there will be neither art nor philosophy, just the perpetual caretaking of the museum of human history. I can feel in myself, and see in others around me, a powerful nostalgia for the time when history existed.' These three lines, combined with the residue of the museum and the smell of autumn and fading light of day, succeeded in inducing a state of nostalgic melancholy that I found wonderfully intoxicating.

As I walked home through the illuminated night air, I thought of Nabokov, who pointed out that by mentally projecting oneself forward in time, the present becomes a future memory. This small adjustment transforms the present from ordinary to anachronistic, tinting everything with the colour of memory, a hue of profound beauty for a time irrevocably lost to the past.

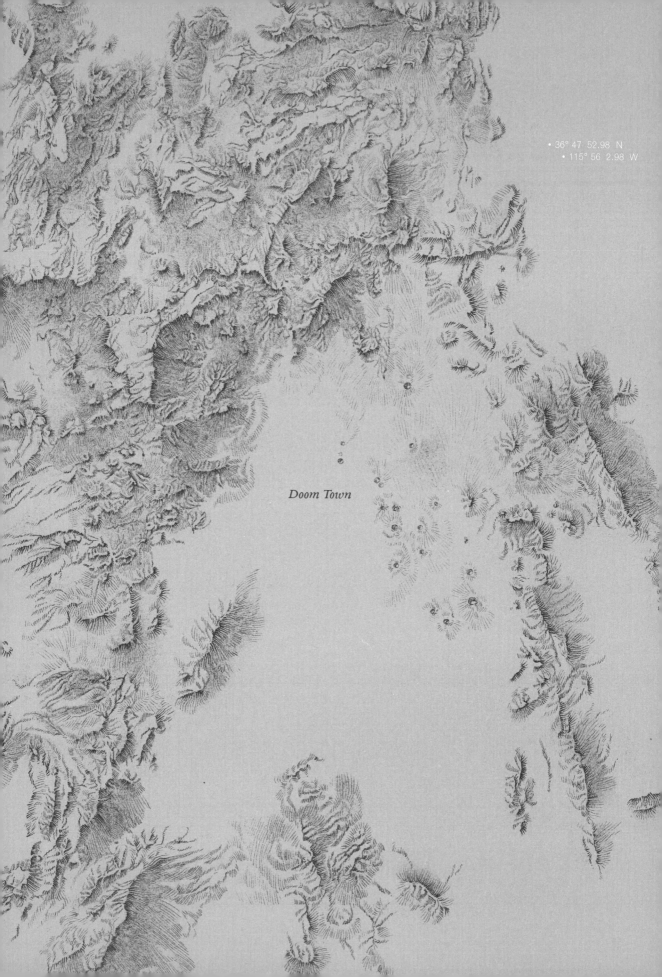

• 36° 47 52.98 N
• 115° 56 2.98 W

Doom Town

Doom Town, Nevada, USA

W**ELCOME TO DOOM TOWN**: the American dream in the heart of the Nevada desert. The 1954 Civil Defense propaganda film *Let's Face It* describes this magical place as made, 'with steel and stone and brick and mortar, with precision and skill – as though it were to last a thousand years. But it is a weird, fantastic city. A creation right out of science fiction. A city like no other on the face of the earth. Homes, neat and clean and completely furnished that will never be occupied. Bridges, massive girders of steel spanning the empty desert. Railway tracks that lead to nowhere, for this is the end of the line.'

On the morning of 5 May 1955 at 5.10am, a 29-kiloton atomic bomb (twice the size of that dropped on Hiroshima) obliterated this cheerful town from the face of the earth. Known to the Civil Defense as Apple II Test Site, to the optimistic as Survival Town and to everyone else as Doom Town, it was designed and built for the sole purpose of destruction. The detonation was just part of numerous operations in which the town was built, destroyed, then rebuilt and re-destroyed like a nightmarish version of Nietzsche's eternal recurrence. It was the quintessential American suburb: along

with a fire and radio station, it had a library, buses and cars, and a dozen homes filled with all-white, smiling, middle-class American families (substituted with mannequins). It was no longer necessary to imagine the destructive havoc of Soviet bombs on American cities – it could now be created. The 'before' photos appear like advertisements from a 1950s *Harper's Bazaar* magazine. In one black-and-white photograph from Operation Doorstep we see two youthful, smartly dressed mannequin couples sitting casually around a kitchen table.

It appears they are about to dine; white porcelain plates and decorative glassware are set neatly across the table's sleek wooden surface. In another 'before' image, we see a different house with a family relaxing in a large, brightly lit living room. On a long, floral-patterned couch a handsome middle-aged man casually reclines. Across from him a tanned and identically dressed man perches on the edge of a chair, his head cocked slightly to one side, as if listening to the man on the couch argue the unfavourable state of the economy. Around them, small children play. To the left of the men a slender, attractive woman sits on a round leather footrest. She is wearing an elegant evening dress. Perhaps they are going to dinner. The fiction unravels when one looks out of the window behind her – not over lush green lawns marked by a white picket fence, but across a bleached desert landscape, an endless expanse that stretches to meet a cloudless Nevada sky. Each of the dozen or so houses was carefully arranged to depict similar dioramic scenes: untroubled children being tucked into bed, archetypal housewives preparing dinner, proud fathers reading the evening paper. What is perhaps most disturbing is the way in which Civil Defense scientists – who could simply have positioned the mannequins in any arbitrary arrangement – intentionally replicated innocent moments of everyday ordinariness, as if to say, this could happen to you *at any moment*.

The 'after' photos deliver on their perversely satisfying promise. The dinner party looks like it has been crashed by a gang of deranged axe murderers – plastic arms and legs lay scattered among shards of wood and broken glass. One man appears reasonably unscathed, until one notices that light shines through coin-sized holes in his head as if it were an ornamental light shade. Surprisingly, the living room of the second house appears only marginally ruined. The coffee table is overturned, the woman by the window has toppled drunkenly backwards, glass fragments and plaster debris litter the floor. While the children have mysteriously disappeared, the man sitting on the chair has not moved at all – as if completely unaware of the nuclear explosion across town, he continues to stare fixedly on an indeterminate point in space, deep in thought.

It is, of course, what happens *between* before and after, the fleeting moment in which the physical world is permanently unmade, that we really want to see. And thanks to stop-motion photography we can. In the 1953 film *Operation Doorstep* our wildest destruction fantasies are realized. 'Here now again is house number one collapsing, shown now in stop-motion,' the narrator announces with considerable pride. We see a blinding light illuminate a moonscape desert, revealing a white timber house standing in the centre of the frame. It spontaneously combusts in black smoke. A moment of calm, followed by an invisible tsunami that tears through the house like a child blowing hundreds of fine white dandelion seeds into the air. 'Remember,' the narrator concludes in a solemn tone, 'what you saw here in detail, happened in just two and one-third seconds.' It is made all the more suspenseful by the dramatic Hitchcockian soundtrack.

It is Eadweard Muybridge, the inventor of stop-motion photography, that we have to thank, at least in part, for making this cinematic experience possible. He was a scientist, innovator and artist; a surgeon of time itself, a taxidermist who captured motion and movement to be dissected and studied. It was in 1878 that Muybridge's famous horse galloped into a future where photography would rapidly become cinema.

We would discover in the next century that to see an atomic blast tear through a house is to watch an autopsy of destruction, in all its slow, glorious and undeniable beauty.

No fewer than 928 atomic bombs were detonated at the Nevada test site between 1951 and 1992. During the 1950s, the tests became a popular tourist attraction. Las Vegas, just 65 miles south-east of the Nevada test site, quickly capitalized on its advantageous location. Dubbed 'Atomic City', Vegas's Chamber of Commerce designed calendars and pamphlets advertising detonation times and prime viewing locations. Hotels and casinos hosted 'Dawn Bomb Parties' where guests sipped 'atomic cocktails' and danced through the night until their very own atomic fireworks show lit up the morning sky. For those unable to witness the dazzling

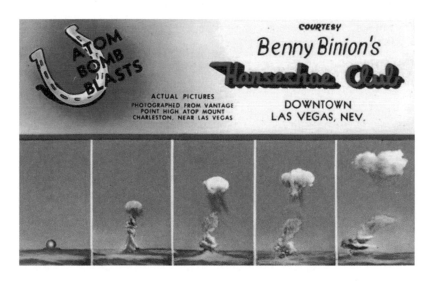

A postcard advertising Benny Binion's Horseshoe Club in Las Vegas.

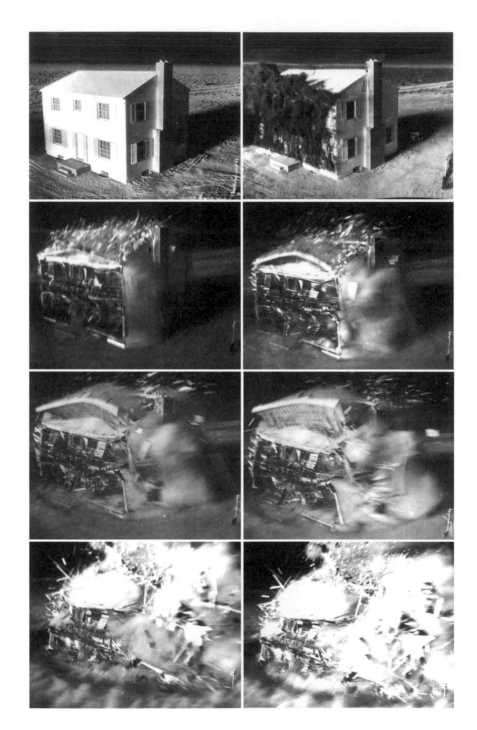

A series of high-speed images captured during Operation Doorstep.

spectacle with their own eyes, tests were frequently broadcast live into homes across the country.

While propaganda films attempted to persuade the public that a nuclear attack was survivable, the public inadvertently discovered the perverse pleasure of witnessing its own self-destruction, cinematically produced and delivered into the comfort of their homes. Given a taste of something we never knew we wanted, there was no putting the destruction genie back in its bottle. Instead, it evolved into the 500-billion-dollar industry that we know today as Hollywood. It is here in the film lots of this strange new city that constructed worlds are routinely annihilated, ever more outrageously apocalyptic scenarios in which we theatrically rehearse our own self-annihilation.

Doom Town was the fictional suburb onto which the anxieties of the future were projected, rewound, replayed, rebuilt and then destroyed once more. Muybridge's primitive stop-motion photography is a retrospective vision of the future in which he showed us how to make the invisible visible. Rebecca Solnit writes of Muybridge, 'He is the man who split the second, as dramatic and far-reaching an action as the splitting of the atom.'

Apocalypse Peaks

Apocalypse Peaks, Antarctica

DURING THE SUMMER of 1958, a group of geology students and staff from New Zealand's Victoria University of Wellington were on their annual Antarctic research trip when, sailing around the protruding outcrop of Victoria Land, they observed four ragged, mountainous peaks against the bleak Antarctic sky. With exceptional imaginative dexterity for geology students, they remarked that the four peaks resembled none other than the Four Horsemen of the Apocalypse. They christened the unnamed mountains the 'Apocalypse Peaks'.

Despite contemporary use of the term to describe an endless array of world-ending calamities, the apocalypse was once exclusively a religious event. The word derives from Greek, meaning to 'reveal' or 'unveil', and refers directly to the Book of Revelation, or the Apocalypse of John. According to most Christians, the biblical apocalypse is a future prophesied by God to end the world with a series of events. Firstly, seven scrolls are opened by 'the Lamb' – a being with no fewer than seven horns and seven eyes – each scroll revealing a depressing future for mankind (except for repentant Christians).

The breaking of the first four seals unleashes the Four Horsemen of the Apocalypse: the white horse conquers, the red horse brings war, the black horse famine and the pale green horse brings death. The opening of the fifth seal reveals the souls of slain martyrs that cry out that God will soon, 'avenge our blood'. When the sixth seal is opened, '...the sky receded like a scroll, rolling up and every mountain and island was removed from its place'. The seventh seal brings half an hour of, 'silence in heaven' followed by the arrival of seven angels, each with a trumpet. This, however, is no musical rendition. As each angel blows its trumpet, a series of calamities is inflicted upon the world. These include (in no particular order) a rain of hail and fire, a five-month plague of horse-sized, human-faced locusts with women's hair, a star named 'Wormwood' that falls from the sky, a mountain of fire that collapses into the sea – annihilating all sea creatures and turning it to blood – destructive earthquakes, and, finally, the extermination of one-third of any thoroughly tormented humans still milling about. The excessiveness of blood, gore and outlandish monsters gives the Book of Revelation the hilarity of a 1980s B-movie horror.

Curiously, while the work is attributed to John, no scholar is actually certain who John is. It is as if the sheer comical outrageousness of the book's content was such that a fictional pen name was needed to conceal the author's true identity.

There are, however, many millions of people today who both fear and eagerly await the biblical apocalypse. A 2012 international poll conducted by Reuters found that nearly 15 per cent of people worldwide believe the world will end during their lifetime. Americans top the chart at 22 per cent, with the British trailing behind at 8 per cent.

For as long as people have populated the world, they have also anticipated its demise. The oldest known apocalyptic prediction dates back to 2800 BC. Assyrian tablets were found to bear the inscription, 'Our Earth is degenerate in these later days; there are signs that the world is speedily coming to an end; bribery and corruption are common; children no longer obey their parents; every man wants to write a book and the end of the world is evidently approaching.'

In 1499, Johannes Stöffler, a respected German mathematician and astrologer, predicted that a biblical flood would consume the earth on 20 February 1524, when all the known planets would align under Pisces, the sign of water. Hundreds of pamphlets announcing the world-ending event were distributed, generating a state of general panic across the country. In one attempt at self-preservation, a German nobleman – Count von Iggleheim – built a luxurious, three-storey ark. The day of reckoning was slightly overcast. When light showers began to fall, hysterical crowds fought for a seat on von Iggleheim's ark, leading to hundreds being killed and von Iggleheim being stoned to death.

For obvious reasons, 1666 was a particularly worrisome year for Christians. For those living in the squalor of London – whose population had already been reduced by one-fifth the year before, thanks to the Black Death – the end times seemed close at hand. On 2 September, a fire broke out in a bakery which raged across London over three days, turning the city into a flaming hell. After some 13,000 buildings and thousands more homes were turned to ash, many saw it as a fulfilment of the apocalypse. In the end, however, the fire claimed only ten lives. While unfortunate, it was not quite the end of the world.

The episode that would become known as the Great Disappointment began during the 1840s when William Miller, a Massachusetts preacher, announced the forthcoming apocalypse. Posters, newsletters and charts circulated his message that the world would end sometime between 21 March 1843 and 21 March 1844. Curiously, in late February 1843, a bright comet appeared in the sky. The Great Comet of 1843 blazed so brightly

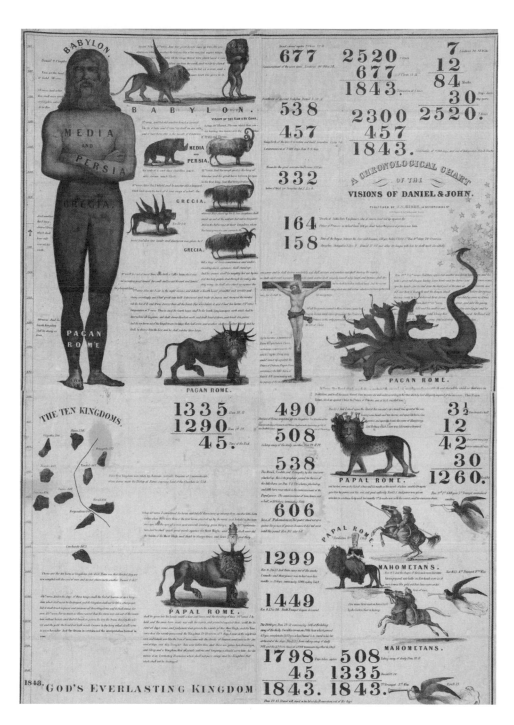

William Miller's 1843 Prophecy Chart.

that for days it could be seen in broad daylight. This ominous sign only served to attract thousands more to the Millerite movement, with as many as 100,000 people discarding their now useless worldly possessions and taking to the surrounding mountains to await the end of the world. When the end failed to arrive, Miller revised the date to 22 October 1844. In the glorious morning sunshine of 23 October, his loyal followers were lamenting once more. One follower, Henry Emmons, wrote, 'I waited all Tuesday and dear Jesus did not come… I lay prostrate for 2 days without any pain, sick with disappointment.'

Perhaps the most prolific of modern apocalyptic predictors was Harold Camping, who publicly announced dates for the end of the world no fewer than twelve times. Based on calculations he made through numbers and dates found in the Bible, in 1992 he published a book titled *1994?* which predicted the end of the world sometime in that year. Perhaps his most infamous prediction was for 21 May 2011, a date he calculated to be exactly seven thousand years after the biblical flood. After the day passed without the appearance of a single horseman, he declared his maths to be off and revised the end of the world to 21 October 2011. 'I'm like the boy who cried wolf again and again and the wolf didn't come,' Camping said. 'This doesn't bother me in the slightest.'

It is not prophets of religion but science that now forecasts the demise of the world. It is not into the sky above they say we should gaze with fearful eyes, but into the Antarctic ice, for earth's destruction will be brought not by a parade of white horses, but by invisible gases. For now, however, we can rest easy. The Four Horsemen of the Apocalypse are still restrained within the azure ice.

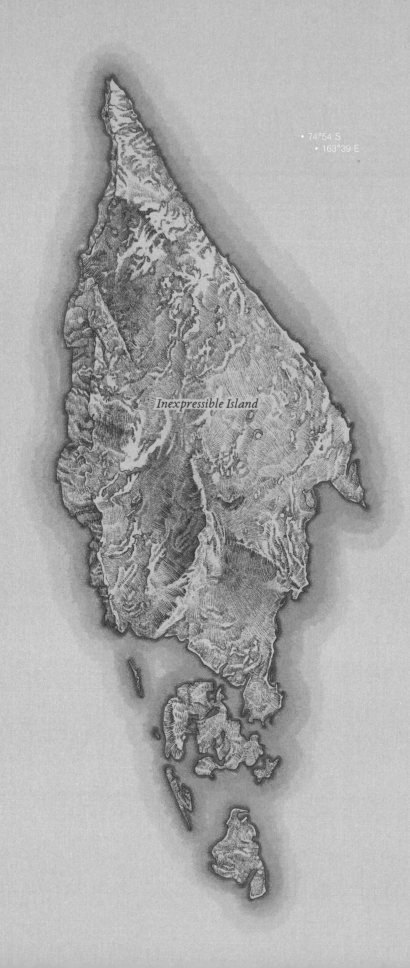

• 74°54 S
• 163°39 E

Inexpressible Island

Inexpressible Island, Antarctica

ANTARCTICA, 1912. 'The road to hell,' wrote George Murray Levick from a small ice cave overlooking a bleak, frozen landscape, 'might be paved with good intentions, but it seemed probable that hell itself would be paved something after the style of Inexpressible Island.' Crippled with dysentery and frostbite, and eating penguins to avoid starvation, the six members of Scott's Terra Nova Expedition found themselves awaiting rescue for a second winter. As with the walls of the cave, Levick had struck against the boundaries of language. Unable to conjure the appropriate word to effectively describe this uncharted and profound strain of misery, he simply named the place 'Inexpressible Island'.

How does one express the inexpressible? Aldous Huxley thought that, after silence, it was music. Johann Wolfgang von Goethe said that art was the mediator of the inexpressible. Rainer Maria Rilke on the other hand believed that, '…most events are inexpressible and take place in a sphere that no word has ever entered'.

Levick wasn't the first person to experience difficulty in expressing this continent. Long before it was sighted in 1820, Antarctica's existence was merely hypothetical, a geographical abstraction. Aristotle first proposed that the continents in the north must be balanced by a landmass in the south. This suggestion naturally gave rise to questions. How big was this land? What was it like? Who or what inhabited it? Such thoughts occupied the imagination of Europeans for centuries. They dreamed of their doppelgängers at the bottom of the world, antipodean civilizations as strange and as opposite as their own. The word antipodes comes from the Greek *antipous*, meaning 'with feet opposite (one's own feet)', from *anti* 'opposed' and *pous* 'foot'. In the years preceding the Enlightenment, ideas of antipodean humans were taken extremely literally. Such imagined civilizations were not merely geographically opposite, but also anatomically reversed, a confused and jumbled arrangement of limbs and extremities. The purely hypothetical land became the projection of countless fears and desires, a place populated by a variety of real and imaginary animals, mutated humans, hideous and demonic creatures who walked upside down. The unseen continent was imagined through stories and myths. Its ideal placelessness became favoured among writers, who constructed speculative works of satirical utopias, dystopias and bizarre imaginings that could all be safely invented without fear of fact or contradiction. Gabriel de Foigny's 1676 work *The Southern Land, Known* features a land populated with antipodean hermaphrodites. Nicolas-Edme Rétif's *Austral Discovery by a Flying Man*, from 1781, includes the utopia 'Megapatagonia' in which, '…all is upside-down and back-to-front'. In Bishop Joseph Hall's novel *Another World and Yet the Same*, published in 1607, the narrator visits a variety of cold, mountainous places, each more terrible than the last. Some are inhabited by lonely people who meet only on Thursdays, hiding indoors where they spend their days, '…imagining and conceiving what was never done and never will be done'. Yet another, modern example is Valery Bryusov's 1905 novel *The Republic of the Southern Cross* which describes an antipodean city afflicted by *mania contradicens,* or 'the disease of contradiction'. Those who succumb to the malady find themselves shouting insults when intending to compliment, or even killing those they wished to help.

An engraving from the 1544 book *Cosmographia*, an imaginary catalogue of peoples of the earth.

Likewise, no one could agree on what this theoretical place actually looked like. When it found its way onto medieval and Renaissance maps between the 16th and 18th centuries, each cartographer expressed the size, shape and geography of the continent according to his own whimsical imaginings. Gerard de Jode's 1578 world map *Universi Orbis seu Terreni Globi* depicts the world as a strange sagging pancake, with *Terra Australis Incognita* shown to be extending as far north as New Guinea. A 1570 map by Abraham Ortelius has *Terra Australis Nondum Cognita* filling almost all of the southern hemisphere, an immense white hand cradling the earth.

When explorers finally began to explore Antarctica during the mid-19th century, it wasn't inverted demonic monsters they had to face, but something far more elusive, shapeless and intangible – the place itself. On this vast, monochromatic landscape – as featureless as it is endless – registers for location, scale and distance are all but absent. Antarctica is a landscape in perpetual flux. Glaciers melt and refreeze. Ice packs extend the land then subtract it. Like a ghost, uncertain of its own existence, shifting, reforming, adjusting, pulsating – it resists shape and form, haunting the imagination.

Hence came the difficulties in exploring, mapping and naming a place more frequently defined by what it isn't than what it is. Even after this illustrious land had been discovered, it evaded definition and defied

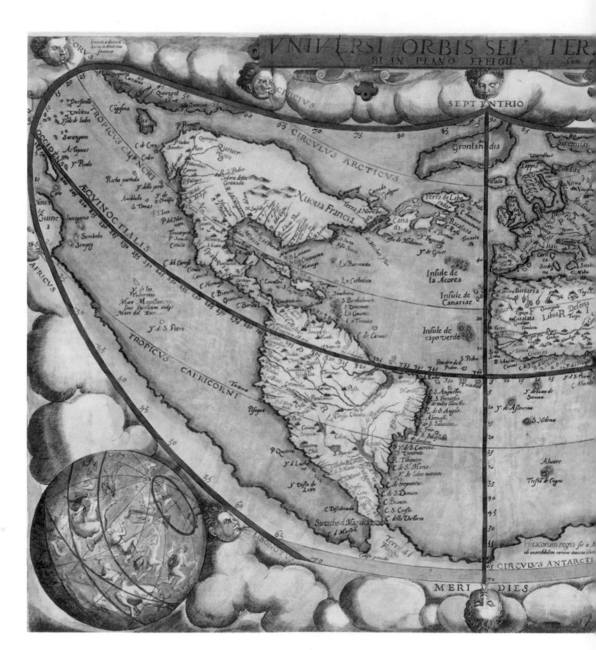

Universi Orbis seu Terreni Globi, Gerard de Jode (1578).

expression. Shapeless Mountain was named thus because none of the exploring party could agree on its shape. So shapeless is Shapeless Mountain that when a later expedition attempted to climb it, they scaled the wrong mountain entirely – which they then named in turn Mistake Mountain. There is also a Wrong Peak, which earned its name under similar circumstances. In 1963, Recoil Glacier was named by a geologist who was said to have physically 'recoiled in disgust' at finding nothing of interest there.

Jorge Luis Borges's *Parable of the Palace* describes a poet who writes a poem about an emperor's immense and beautiful palace. The poet's brief composition (some say it consisted of a single word) described the palace so perfectly that the enraged emperor exclaimed, 'You have robbed me of my palace!' and had the poet immediately executed. The parable continues, and in some versions the palace vanished entirely when the poem was recited as, 'There cannot be any two things alike in the world; the poet, they say, had only to utter his poem to make the palace disappear, as if abolished and blown to bits by the final syllable.' So effective was the representation that it replaced that which it sought to represent. Where Antarctica's maps and mythologies failed in accurate representation, they instead succeeded in creating a haunting double, a place that existed not at the bottom of the world, but in the depths of the imagination.

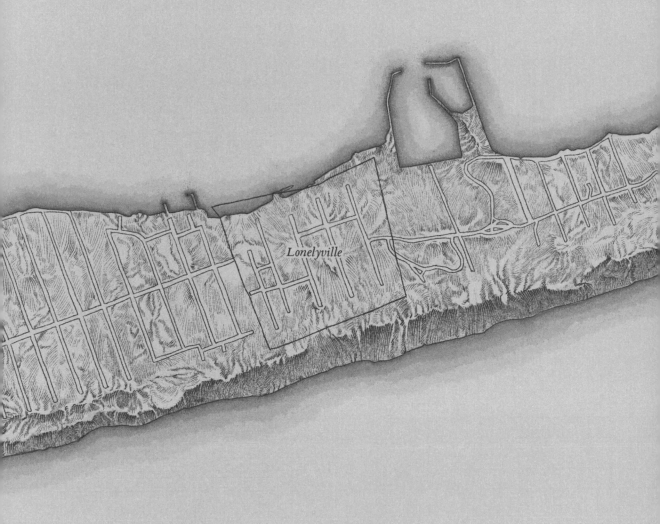

Lonelyville

Lonelyville, New York, USA

THE LAWS OF Lonelyville were set down in writing: 'No person or persons not of good moral character shall be permitted to dwell within the city limits. The Sabbath day shall be strictly observed by every person in sound health taking a bath. There shall be no horse racing, cock fights or firemen's tournaments on Sundays. No wild animals such as lions, tigers, elephants, porpoises or whales shall be kept within the city limits.' And finally, 'The board of Aldermen shall be responsible that shall see that the tide rises and falls every day and that the surf continues to roll in.' And with that, the parliament and community of Lonelyville, consisting entirely of three men, voted unanimously in favour of their own proposed laws.

Lonelyville lies in the east of the thirty-two-mile strip of land that is Fire Island. Running parallel to and roughly four miles off Long Island, New York, Fire Island holds a rather tenuous geographic status, more permanent sandbar than island, its topography continually being reshaped in relation to both weather and climate.

The island, which had been used as a whaling hub until the late 17th century, did not actually gain its first resident until a man named Jeremiah Smith built a cottage next to the beach there in 1795. According to island mythology, Smith spent his days coaxing unsuspecting ships to shore, murdering their crews and looting their supplies. Smith's mischievous activities weren't, however, the only untoward enterprises taking place on the island. Slave traders used the island's inhospitable geography to hold and torture their captives and, later, rumrunners stashed their precious liquids among the dunes and trees. Fortunately, things have improved on the island in more recent history. This started in earnest in 1880 when a restaurant was opened, eventually evolving into the community of Cherry Grove. Its appearance would signal the arrival of future development across the island. In the 1890s, resorts and other

communities began springing up, beginning with Chautauqua Assembly, an oddly popular Christian movement at the time. The island began to possess a life and culture of its own, gaining lustre and allure, especially for those seeking a change or refuge from city life. In the early 1900s, developers purchased tracts of land which they resold as vacation lots to wealthy city dwellers looking to escape New York City. The island's emergence as an ineluctable destination point was intractable. Over time, the slender island divided into small autonomous communities, each possessing a distinct demography and identity.

It was in the summer of 1908 that three friends – Harry Brewster, an ex-Justice of the Peace; Harry Raven, an ex-bank cashier; and Selah Clock, an ex-tax collector – together purchased a lot of empty land on the island. Paying homage to their sur-

names, they respectively called their three modest beach shacks Brewster's Bungalow, Raven's Ranch and Clock's Castle. The men spent their summers, '…killing ducks… catching "suckers" and other things out in the bay when there is nothing else to do, and between intervals of sleep, dining at the expense of each other and swapping stories'. It was at one such dinner that Brewster, '…racked his fertile brain for a name for the collection of "shanties" at the beach colony, and almost immediately "Lonelyville" suggested itself'. And, as the story goes, '…with due éclat and champagne, the resort was christened and launched upon the sea of fame'.

Lonelyville progressively grew from a lonesome collection of beach shanties into a populated community. In 1963, renowned comedian Mel Brooks and his partner Anne Bancroft bought a shingle-clad beachfront house on No Name Walk, designed by famed American artist and architect Richard Meier. Brooks, who surely appreciated the dark hilarity of his community's founding fathers, hosted parties at the house in which he would amuse his guests with improv comedy routines. It was at one such party that Mel

LONELYVILLE · BY · THE · BAY.

Sketched by an Artist as Yet Unknown to Fame.

An early sketch of Lonelyville around 1908.

Brooks and Carl Reiner came up with the idea for a sketch called 'The 2000-year-old Man'. It eventually evolved into a 1970s television show in which Reiner questioned Brooks on what it's like to be 2,000 years old. Brooks then formulated witty replies from the perspective of one who has witnessed the unfolding of history.

Always susceptible to the rampaging forces of nature, Fire Island was struck by Hurricane Sandy in 2012. The storm wreaked havoc, levelling homes and submerging parts of the island under several feet of ocean water. Those who lived there were made painfully aware of the island's low-lying topographic vulnerability. What transpired on Fire Island can be seen as both

prophetic and emblematic of the processes occurring in the world at large. There are climate scientists who insist that Hurricane Sandy is yet another ominous sign of global warming, and who predict that in as little as 200 years, Lonelyville, as well as all low-lying geography across the globe, will become part of the ever-growing ocean floor.

'Comedy is about truth, it's about failure,' writes comedian Holly Burn, '…it deals with the fall of man and the human condition, it helps us understand ourselves and the world we live in.' By assuming the impossible perspective of a 2,000-year-old man, Brooks plays to the fundamental comic mathematics that says comedy equals tragedy plus time. From Brooks's ancient perspective, human history appears as little more than a succession of mishaps, an epic tragi-comedy in which humankind, helpless and blundering, plays the lead role, a slapstick production set in the theatre of the world. 'Tragedy is when I cut my finger,' Brooks once said. 'Comedy is when you fall into an open sewer and die.' If we are, as climate scientists warn, poised on the precipice of the open sewer that is global warming, then it will be not tragedy, but comedy when Lonelyville lies at the bottom of the sea.

Mel Brooks and Anne Bancroft's Lonelyville beach house in 1963.
Image courtesy of Ricahrd Meier & Partners Architects.

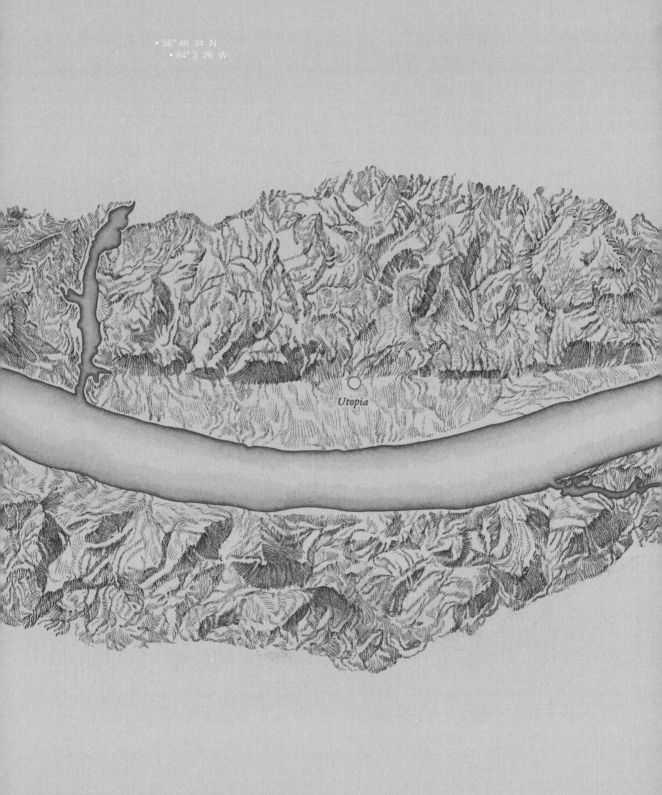

38° 46 34 N
84° 3 26 W

Utopia

Utopia, Ohio, USA

EVERY UTOPIA HAS an implied dystopia. The irrestible idea of a perfect society is an ancient one, perhaps even as old as society itself. The word utopia can be traced back to its first appearance as the title of the 1516 novel by Sir Thomas More. In his visionary tale, More imagined an island named Utopia on which its inhabitants lived in perfect, social harmony. Utopia was antithetical with Europe and possessed everything it lacked – religious freedom, collective ownership, education for all. There was gender equality and everyone enjoyed meaningful work. More's utopian vision grew out of and was in stark contrast to the harsh religious austerity afflicting Europe during the pre-Enlightenment period. Like many, More was inspired by the voyages of Christopher Columbus who, little more than twenty years earlier, had discovered the New World and, with it, unleashed the real possibility of a new and perfect society. Yet, even before the word utopia appeared, utopian societies, if only imaginary, had long existed. From the Garden of Eden, to Plato's *Republic*, *The Land of Cockaigne* and Bacon's *New Atlantis*, these places suggest that if paradise has been lost, its loss is not irrevocable. When Columbus encountered the New World and its indigenous inhabitants, he believed he had found the elusive Garden of Eden.

Then, around the middle of the 20th century, several novels again reshaped the way we imagined the future. George Orwell's *1984*, Aldous Huxley's *Brave New World* and Ray Bradbury's *Fahrenheit 451*, all written just before or after the rise and fall of the Third Reich, are not hopeful visions of an idealistic future, but ominous warnings of human corruption and social decay. They are cautionary tales against the utopian search, for the sole reason that such a search, as history has shown, can only lead to tyrannical dictatorship – in other words, dystopia.

As immigrants began to filter into the New World, they found it more palatable to rely on collective rather than individual effort, and so various small communities began to appear along the frontier. Many of those who had fled Europe to escape religious persecution now initiated their own micro-societies, where the freedom to construct a life – one only previously imagined – was at least now possible. Led by charismatic leaders, these communities formed around idealistic principles and a new religious freedom. Showing the popularity and range of this arrangement, by 1900 more than 100 utopian communities were established all across North America.

Charles Fourier, the French philosopher and early socialist thinker, had built a dedicated following in North America. Fourier believed in collective cooperation, with his utopian vision taking the form of small autonomous societies that he called 'phalanxes'. A society formed around gender equality, mutual investment, collective living and labour would, Fourier asserted, experience higher productivity and individual happiness. One could be content, as jobs within the society would be assigned based on one's own interests and desires. Higher pay would be given for jobs deemed universally undesirable, such as ploughing fields (or potentially undertaken by Jewish slaves who Fourier believed to be 'the source of evil'). Fourier insisted that communal living was essential and for this he designed an enormous structure he called a *phalanstère*. The architectural plan of the *phalanstère* consisted of three areas; a central section and two lateral wings. The building would be replete with private apartments, a dining and meeting room, libraries, along with a school, ballroom, workshop and playroom.

In Fourier's utopia, social harmony was guaranteed by assembling exactly 1,620 members, since he believed there were just twelve common passions that resulted in 810 types of character. In this way, every possible want, need and desire could be duly satisfied. It would be a society free of government, unfettered capitalism and the oppressive labour exploitation Fourier saw as the scourge of the modern world. While many of Fourier's ideas seemed lucid and even viable, others appeared completely severed from reality. Among such ideas, Fourier believed that his utopian world would last 80,000 years (a period in which six moons would orbit the earth), that there would be 37 million poets equal to Homer, that the North Pole would become milder than the Mediterranean (perhaps now not completely inconceivable), the seas would desalinate and turn to lemonade, and that every woman would have no fewer than four husbands.

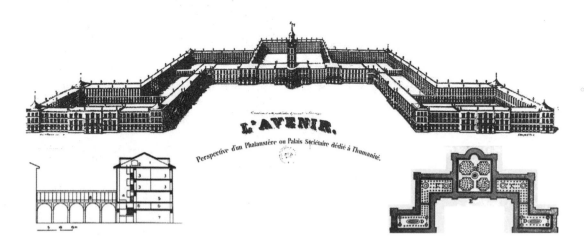

Perspective view and architectural plan of Fourier's *phalanstère*.

While Fourier may have been overreaching in some of his predictions, he nevertheless gained a strong following. In 1844, seven years after Fourier's death, a group of dedicated followers collectively purchased a plot of land along the Ohio River to build a new and idealistic community based on his teachings. They called their new society 'Utopia'. The community drew new families to move there, and for an annual fee of $25, each would receive a timber house and a portion of land. After only two years, however, the society fell apart. Its members, impatient for the 80,000 years of Perfect Harmony to begin, grew disillusioned and, as people left, the community went bankrupt.

In 1847, John Wattles, a charismatic spiritualist leader, purchased the land and brought his 100 followers to Utopia. It was the perfect location for the spiritualist society – an isolated stretch of 1,400 acres along the Ohio River where they could live free from the intrusions of modern society. They fused traditional Christian beliefs with a new spiritualism, and practised strict vegetarianism and temperance. Wattles was a follower of 'harmonial philosophy', a belief system developed by Andrew Jackson Davis, a charismatic Mesmerist, magnetic healer and clairvoyant. In 1847, Davis published *The Principles of Nature, Her Divine Revelations*. Heavily influenced by the socialist writings of Fourier, Davis wrote about the existence of utopian worlds on distant planets, in-

habited by supremely intelligent, attractive and virtuous individuals. Davis blended his own ideas with Fourier's theories of reincarnation, asserting the likelihood of being reincarnated as a superior being on another planet, or more curiously, as another planet.

Shortly after the spiritualists had settled into Utopia, they decided to move the town hall, brick by brick, closer to the banks of the Ohio River. On 13 December 1847, merely days after the move was complete, heavy rains caused a flash flood to surge down the river in what would prove to be one of the worst floods of the 19th century.

A spiritualist phograph by William Hope, circa 1920.

By unfortunate chance, the town's residents were in the hall celebrating when the flood struck; the surge of water tore the hall apart, emphatically ruining the celebration and sweeping everyone downstream. While some survived, most drowned or were killed by hypothermia from the icy water.

'All accounts speak of the killed persons of the highest moral worth,' read a local newspaper shortly after the flood, 'devoting all their energies to the cause of human happiness and progression.' While Utopia didn't descend into an Orwellian dystopia, it did fail, due to circumstances beyond its control, to bring to fruition the promise of its idealistic name. The word utopia originates from Greek, meaning *ou-topos*: no-place. It seems fitting that Utopia should return to an abstract and unrealized ideal. After all, it is an idea that contains within it the paradoxical promise of non-existence. But perhaps it does exist. One needs to look no further than the social and economic disparities in modern-day America to realize that one person's utopia is another's dystopia.

• 40°38 31 S
  • 144°43 33 E

Cape Grim

Suicide Bay

Cape Grim, Tasmania, Australia

ers scrambled around the cliff and what remained the monsters put to death. Those poor creatures who had sought shelter in the cleft of the rock they forced to the brink of an awful precipice, massacred them all and threw their bodies down the precipice.'

It was only twenty-five years earlier, in 1803, that Lieutenant John Bowen, under orders from Governor Philip King, sailed to the unexplored island to the south of the Australian continent and established an outpost on its eastern shore. The island was called Van Diemen's Land, having been named by the Dutch who had first discovered it some years earlier. Its vast, rugged terrain, together with its insurmountable topography, rendered it the perfect place to send incoming ships loaded with convicts from England. While difficult prisoners found themselves relegated to the notorious Port Arthur Penal Colony, most served out their sentences as labourers assigned to free settlers, companies and civil construction projects. In 1826, the Van Diemen's Land Company established itself on the island and was awarded some 250,000 acres of land in the north-west to farm merino and Saxon sheep. It was, to both the company and the government, of little consequence that the land was not vacant but already occupied and home to several Aboriginal tribes. Despite this, company ships began arriving, delivering sheep and convicts for labour. Not satisfied with merely commandeering the land, within just one year the Van

F EBRUARY 10, 1828. A summer's morning, the air was cool and the sea calm. One kilometre offshore, two rocky formations sprouted from the sea, their sheer cliffs ascending to lush green tops. The Aboriginal women ventured out into the waves. Foamy sea water encircled their naked bodies as they swam together out to the islands. On shore, the rest of the tribe collected firewood to feed the campfires, from which thin columns of smoke drifted skywards. After several hours, the women re-emerged from the waves. In their hands they carried wet bundles of mutton birds captured from the islands, their legs bound together with grass to form feathery bouquets. The seventy or so members of the Peerapper tribe at last gathered around the campfires to feast on the catch. It was then that the thunderous crack of musket fire shattered the clear morning air. Chaos erupted. Bodies ran and darted, no one knowing which direction to turn. 'Some rushed into the sea,' George Augustus Robinson wrote in 1830, '…oth-

Diemen's Land Company earned itself a notorious reputation for its brutal treatment of the local Aboriginals.

The attack on the Peerapper tribe – in which some thirty Aboriginal men were slaughtered – was perpetrated by four men from the Van Diemen's Land Company. The incident, which has subsequently become known as the Cape Grim Massacre, merely constituted a single act of violence in the ongoing war between natives and settlers across the entire island. In fact, as more settlers and convicts arrived, incidents of bloody violence soared. Sex-deprived convicts kidnapped, raped and murdered Aboriginal women and girls. Tribes responded with guerrilla-style attacks, only to provoke murderous reprisals by the settlers.

We can turn to 19th century theories of scientific racism to partly explain the collective lack of concern surrounding the unfolding genocide of the native population, not just in Van Diemen's Land, but across all of Australia. When Charles Darwin travelled to Australia in January 1836, he naively considered that some 'mysterious agency' was responsible for the rapid extinction of the Australian Aboriginal race, observing in *The Voyage of the Beagle* that, '…the varieties of man seem to act on each other in the same way as different species of animals – the stronger always extirpating the weaker'. His unfortunate correlation between animal and human was appropriated as scientific

evidence to support England's imperial conquest over Australia's native population. The term 'social Darwinism' was coined, implying that primitive races were inferior to the 'civilized' nations of the West. Indigenous cultures, it was believed, were evolutionarily backwards; races of people already destined for extinction. The British, it was believed, were merely hastening the inevitable. 'Whether the Blacks deserve any mercy at the hands of the pioneering squatters is an open question,' wrote Harold Finch-Hatton, an early Australian federationist, 'but that they get none is certain. They are a doomed race, and before many years they will be completely wiped out of the land.' English writer Anthony Trollope thought the Australian Aboriginals to be, '…ineradicably savage, of a sapient monkey imitating the gait and manners of a do-nothing white dandy,' asserting later that, '…it is their fate to be abolished; and they are already vanishing'. To the Victorian imperialist mind, it was 'survival of the fittest', evidence of Darwin's Theory of Evolution in action. 'Wherever the European has trod,' Darwin himself observed, 'death seems to pursue the Aboriginal.'

Amid escalating violence in Van Diemen's Land from both sides, evangelical settler George Augustus Robinson was appointed as conciliator between the settlers and Aboriginals. Just as he was arriving on the island in 1824, Lieutenant-Governor

George Arthur had declared martial law, even awarding bounties (five pounds for adults and two pounds for children) for the capture and killing of any Aboriginals. What eventually became known as the Black War claimed the lives of fewer than 200 settlers but eventually resulted in the annihilation of the island's entire Aboriginal population.

Robinson, sympathetic to the Aboriginal struggle, investigated the massacre at Cape Grim. He determined it to be the final incident in a series of escalating and vengeful acts that had begun months earlier, when men from the Van Diemen's Land Company had attempted to lure several Aboriginal girls into their hut. A fight erupted, which left one worker with a spear through his leg and several Aboriginal men dead. In retaliation, a number of tribesmen rounded up the company's sheep flock and drove them off a cliff; incidentally, the same cliff over which their own bodies would later be thrown.

The Governor of Van Diemen's Land ordered Robinson to round up the last remaining Aboriginals on Van Diemen's Land and convince them to resettle on Flinders Island, a small island in the Bass Strait. Robinson quickly agreed, seeing the rapid extermination of the Aboriginal population as otherwise inevitable. Together with an Aboriginal man named Truganini, Robinson succeeded in convincing almost all of the native population to move to Flinders

Island with a promise of food, housing and security until the situation on the mainland had calmed down. By the end of 1835, nearly all the Aboriginals of Van Diemen's Land had been successfully relocated.

Robinson's well-intentioned effort to save the remaining Aboriginals would, however, prove to be their death sentence. Once on Flinders Island, he ordered them to undergo a programme that would render them, 'civilised and Christianised'. Forbidden to practise traditional customs, they were forced to wear clothes and were given European names. Men were made to clear land, shear sheep, build roads and fences, while women had to wash clothes and attend sewing classes. As conditions rapidly deteriorated, Flinders Island transformed into a kind of prison camp rather than the sanctuary Robinson had promised. Robinson quickly grew disillusioned with his project and abandoned the island. Diseases spread, killing most of the native population. In 1847, with only forty-seven people left, the Aboriginals were again moved, this time to Oyster Cove, south of Hobart.

'At some future period,' wrote Darwin in *The Descent of Man*, 'not very distant as measured by centuries, the civilized races of man will almost certainly exterminate and replace throughout the world the savage races.' Before European settlers arrived in 1803, Van Diemen's Land had been home to an estimated 7,000 Aboriginals, who had occupied the island for some 40,000 years. By 1905, just over a century later, not one was left.

It was Walter Benjamin who coined the maxim, 'history is written by the victors'. Indeed, it is not the victims, but the victors who get to create their own self-written historicism, a story that, in time, becomes the story of the epoch. On maps and in documents of Van Diemen's Land, the cliff over which the thirty bodies of the Peerapper tribe were thrown became labelled as Victory Hill. The rocky beach beneath the cliff was named Suicide Bay. 'There is no document of civilization,' wrote Benjamin, 'which is not at the same time a document of barbarism.' In 1856, Van Diemen's Land, in an attempt to rid itself of associations with its dark past, was renamed Tasmania.

GOVERNOR DAVEY'S PROCLAMATION TO THE ABORIGINES 1816.

"Why Massa Gubernor", said Black Jack .. "You Proclamation all gammon"
"How Blackfellow read him eh ? He no learn him read book."
"Read that then" said the Governor, pointing to a picture

Proclamation to the Aborgines, 1816. Governor George Arthur's board shows a four-strip pictogram that visually explains the idea of equality under the law.
Image courtesy of the Mitchell Library, State Library of New South Wales.

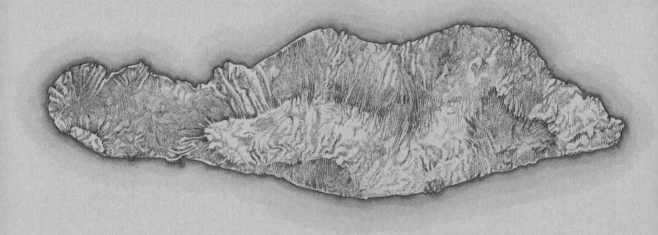

Massacre Island

Massacre Island, Ontario, Canada

FEW OBJECTS ARE as emblematic of the 18th century as the black felt top hat. First surging in popularity across European salons towards the end of the 16th century, the iconic fashion accessory came to adorn the heads of men everywhere for a solid 200 years. More than just an essential component of a fashionable wardrobe, it was through one's hat that wealth, status and social standing were communicated.

It reflected everything important about a man; his income and occupation, and even his political and religious affiliations. While it mattered little if the hat was worn or simply toted underarm, it became an essential carry item for any dignified gentleman. A man without a hat was a man without status. The top hat, which was also known as a high hat, stovepipe, chimney pot or simply topper, took not one, but several archetypal forms, depending on the image its owner wished to convey. There was the standard Regent, refined yet candid; the dignified d'Orsay; the flared Wellington with its orange-skin curled brim. The Paris Beau was favoured by dandies, with its

Shapes and styles of beaver felt hats from 1776 to 1825.

whimsical inverted cone, often ornamented with a single white feather. Regardless of the particular style of the hat, it was, beyond colour and shape, the hat's material that mattered most in determining its ultimate worth. Sheep, rabbit, fox, mink, otter or even bear were fine options for crafting felt, yet nothing compared to the sheer elegance of silky yet durable Canadian beaver fur. A single top hat required no less than two kilograms of beaver pelt to create. The soft underhair was shaved from the skin and combined with various adhesives; the resulting material was matted, steamed and moulded over a hat-form block and then forged into the desired shape. Mercury was a common adhesive ingredient, which often poisoned unsuspecting hatmakers, giving rise to the expression to be 'mad as a hatter'.

The immense popularity of this idiosyncratic, and surprisingly impractical, male headdress in Europe drove the demand for beaver pelts in North America. Native tribes of the northern regions, who had hunted and trapped beaver for generations, now capitalized on the new trade economy. They bartered the pelts with French settlers and European traders – not for money, but goods. The fur trade quickly became the driving force behind the European exploration of the uncharted wilderness that blanketed the north of the continent. With overland travel notoriously slow and fraught with danger, the search for nautical routes began. Unsubstantiated rumours spread throughout the French colonies and trading posts about the existence of an im-mense inland sea to the west of the North American continent. Said to be as large as Hudson's Bay or the Gulf of Mexico, many believed that it began at the Pacific Ocean and flowed east, penetrating deep into the continent. This mythical inland sea was dubbed by the French as the *Mer de l'Ouest,* or the Sea of the West. Shortly after the hypothetical *Mer de l'Ouest* began to ap-pear on maps, the French explorer and fur trader Pierre Gaultier de Varennes, sieur de La Vérendrye offered to substantiate its existence. With funding provided by the

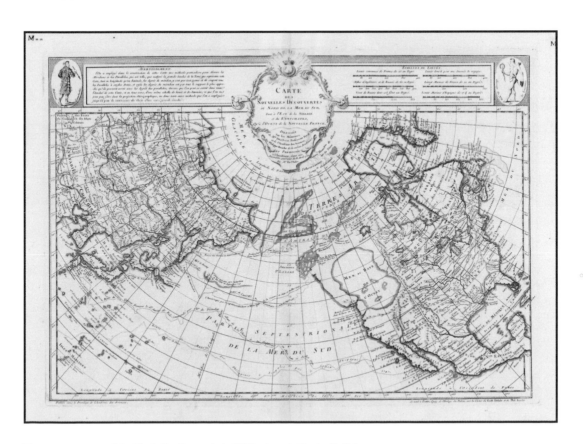

The erroneous map of the North Pacific, made in 1752 by Joseph Nicolas Delisle, shows '*Mer ou Baye de l'Ouest*', or the mythical Sea of the West.

fur trade, La Vérendrye (together with his three teenage sons, Jean-Baptiste, Pierre and François) left Montreal on 26 August 1731, alongside an exploration party of some fifty men.

Through dense, rugged terrain, they pushed west on horseback, establishing new fur-trading posts along their way. The following year, having made it only halfway across the continent, the exploration party founded a trading post on Lake of the Woods, which they christened Fort Saint-Charles. During this era, Lake of the Woods was the centre of a fierce conflict zone between several indigenous tribes, namely the Cree, Teton-Lakota, Sioux, Dakota and Ojibwa tribes, all forming alliances with each other and European traders in a complex and tenuously balanced relationship of war, peace and trade.

Several years passed before La Vérendrye continued west with his party, leaving his son Jean-Baptiste in Fort Saint-Charles to help manage the newly established trading post. On the afternoon of 5 June 1736, Jean-Baptiste and twenty other Frenchmen set off from Fort Saint-Charles in three large timber canoes heading for the communities of Kaministiquia and Michilimackinac to buy supplies and provisions. However, by the end of the following day, the group had inexplicably failed to arrive. The day after that, a group of travellers arrived at Fort Saint-Charles by canoe, yet ominously they

too had not seen any trace of the men. A search was launched and it did not take long before Jean-Baptiste and his companions were found. That following day, the search party arrived at a small island in the east of the lake. After landing their canoes, they walked into a small forest clearing, where, in the centre of the island, they found the twenty-one men and a horrific scene.

They were, '…lying in a circle against one another', recalled one of the men from the search party. Their decapitated heads lay beside them, carefully wrapped like morbid gifts in beaver skins. Jean-Baptiste, '…was stretched on the ground, face downward, his back all hacked with a knife; there was a large opening in his loins and his headless trunk was decked out with garters and bracelets of porcupine quills'. The murderers were never found and instead the French fur traders were left struggling to decipher meaning from the gruesome scene and the cryptic adornment of the dismembered corpses.

It was, above all, the gesture of wrapping the heads in beaver skins that unsettled the French. Perhaps it was a symbol of resentment towards the Europeans for their insatiable lust for beaver fur, a lust that was quickly driving the species to extinction. Perhaps the absurdity of the gesture was meant to echo the absurdity of what the beaver skins were destined to become: symbolic adornments for the heads of European men concerned with little more than the acquisition of power, status and wealth.

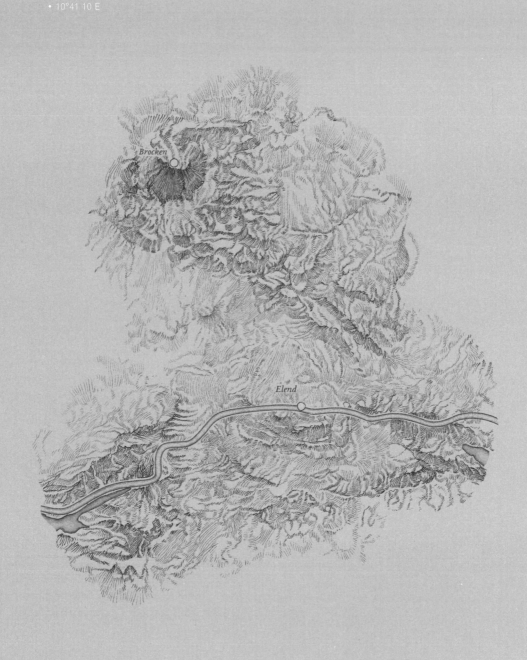

Misery (Elend), Saxony-Anhalt, Germany

rumoured site of witches and demonic rituals since the 17th century, featuring in some of Germany's greatest art and literature. On *Walpurgisnacht*, an annual occurrence on the night of 30 April, it's said that the world's witches meet on its peak for the orgy that damned Goethe's Faust.

Goethe lived in Misery during the summer of 1784, exploring the Harz mountains, in particular Brocken, which looms over the meek village bellow. Goethe was especially enchanted by the strange granite pillars and outcrops that had given the mountain its occult reputation – possessing landmarks with such names as 'The Devil's Wall', 'Devil's Pulpit' or 'Witches' Altar'. With the mountain already established as an ancient site of satanic ritual, Goethe reformed it into a pantheistic Romantic vision of God and nature as one, using the Witches' Altar as the famed setting for Faust to witness the spectacle of *Walpurgisnacht*. Goethe's intense interest, if not obsession, for the granite evolved into an essay titled 'Über den Granit' or 'On Granite', which he composed in his cottage in Misery. The part-geological enquiry, part-lyrical meditation on nature posits, however incorrectly, granite to be *the* primordial rock, the foundation on which all else stands – an uninterrupted vein flowing back to the very beginnings of time itself. It became for Goethe the grandest symbol of a lost and primordial world. 'Sitting on a high bare peak,' wrote Goethe, 'looking down

MISERY LIES AT the heart of Germany. This Arcadian village, ensconced in a darkened landscape of forests and granite mountains, lies in a region rich in mythology and legends, many of which were collected by the Brothers Grimm during the early 19th century as, '...fragments of belief dating back to the most ancient times'. Misery sits at the foot of Brocken – 'Broken Mountain', the highest peak of the Harz mountains. Generations of hikers and mountaineers have reported an enormous looming figure following them in the mist, a ghostly image surrounded by radiating circles of light. The phenomenon, known as the Brocken Spectre, was first reported by the naturalist Johann Silberschlag in 1780. In reality, the spectre is simply the hiker's own shadow being projected onto the clouds by an uncanny play of mountain light. Brocken, however, is no ordinary peak. Steeped in folklore and mythology, it's been a

A black magic experiment atop Brocken on Goethe's birthday in 1932.
The goal was to transform a goat into a young man. It proved unsuccessful.

racial 'science' and ancient purity – a purity not of stone, but blood. Even from Brocken's boundless view, Goethe could not have envisioned the dark future that lay just over the horizon, the haphazard mountains of ruin that would come to separate his virtuous world from the impending destruction to come.

upon a vast region, I'm able to say to myself: you are right on top of a foundation which goes to the very heart of the earth…no haphazard pile of ruins separates you from the firm surface of the original world itself.'

The ensuing centuries would see Goethe's philosophy on nature and man be appropriated with new vision and meaning, first by the German Romantics and then, in the mid-20th century, the National Socialists. It would be the latter who, with stolen rhetoric, would promise a transformed nation – one that would unite a broken and humiliated people with their fatherland. They preached of a new cultural landscape, one that harked back to a mythical and romanticized past, and one based around *völkisch* ideology of

Granite soon had other admirers. Nazi architect Albert Speer found the stone irresistible, this time as the symbolic building material for the Third Reich's adoption and exploitation of the German Romantic vision. For Speer, granite was force incarnate: both ancient and pure. Both he and Hitler wanted granite, Goethe's primordial stone, to last 1,000 years as architectural marvels of the Third Reich's Romantic vision. German Romanticism was perfectly poised to act as host for the parasitical doctrines of Nazism; namely the fascination with an inner darkness, theatrical death and, perhaps most interestingly, organic ruins. 'Theory of Ruin Value' was an idea put forward by Speer, suggesting that future buildings and monuments should be designed and built ready to embrace

the inevitability of decay; falling gracefully into picturesque ruins, so that even in 1,000 years, they would still be able to, '…communicate the heroic inspirations of the Third Reich'. Speer insisted on natural materials such as granite over concrete, claiming that, like marble, it produced the most unsurpassed aesthetic ruins. 'The ages-old stone buildings of the Egyptians and the Romans,' declared Speer, 'still stand today as powerful architectural proofs of the past of great nations.'

However, aerial bombing would transform the cities of the Third Reich not into the Romantic picturesque ruins Speer had envisioned, but into decimated landscapes of carnage and destruction. In East Germany, one dictatorship gave way to another with the consequence that Goethe's beloved town of Misery found itself on the wrong side of the border, only by several kilometres. The new Communist leaders were less enchanted with the romance of granite, tending instead towards the utilitarian charms of precast concrete. They used it to restore the decimated ruins of East Germany and to construct the Inner Wall, the insidious barrier that would emphatically divide the country in two for the next thirty years. They did, however, find one use for granite. It came in the form of rectangular blocks called *Grenzsteine*, which were embedded into the ground along the West-facing side of the border. The stones, which featured on one side the letters 'DDR' in ominous black type, had the appearance of gravestones prophesying the nation's impending demise.

The East German Inner Wall, overlooking the Harz mountains.

Misery even had the ignominious fate of being the official holiday resort of the notoriously brutal East German secret police – the Stasi – a fact that surely unsettled the locals. In 1972, a young man ran into trees on the edge of the town. Moments later, a rapid blast of machine-gun fire ruptured the night air. East German soldiers found the man's body beside the grey concrete wall. It appeared he had been attempting to flee to the greener pastures of the West. The futility of his death, along with the 125 others who were killed while trying to escape the East, would embody the misery of this period. After reunification in 1989, Misery promptly became a popular destination once more for those from both sides of the former border. Today, during the summer, hikers again wander through Goethe's primordial world, a scarred and transformed landscape in which myths and legend, like granite, still flow back to the very beginning of time itself.

Memory
of the
Nameless

'Being past, being no more, is passionately at work in things.'
WALTER BENJAMIN, *Arcades Project*

'Today I passed Los Angeles and tramped on southwest,' wrote Albert Speer in his diary on 5 September 1965. 'Merciless sun on dusty roads. My soles burned on the hot ground, for months without rain.'

Some years ago I was given a copy of Albert Speer's diary. Published in 1975, it is an assemblage of entries he had smuggled out of prison on scraps of toilet paper and cigarette wrappers over a period of twenty years. Speer, the infamous Nazi architect, spent most of his later life in Berlin's Spandau prison after narrowly avoiding the Nuremberg gallows.

On that day in early September 1965, Speer wasn't tramping past Los Angeles, but was in prison, the same prison where he had been for the past twenty years. In his abundance of free time, Speer had developed the meditative practice of taking long walks around the prison garden. The garden – which he himself had designed and built – was a rambling and elaborate landscape of fruit trees and winding paths, ornamental rock gardens and floral arrangements. He meticulously recorded each lap around the garden by moving peas from one pocket to the other, allowing him to calculate the number of kilometres walked.

One particular day it occurred to him that he could walk an imaginary journey from the prison to his childhood home in Heidelberg, a distance of some 626 kilometres. Each evening after his daily trek, he traced out the distance he travelled around the garden onto a map of Germany that he had borrowed from the prison library. On 19 March 1955, after several weeks of walking, he finally reached Heidelberg. Then Speer had another idea. He wrote to friends, requesting maps and travel guides for the Middle East, Asia and North America. Like a backpacker gearing up for a world tour, he immersed himself in atlases, world maps, history books and travelogues. Over the next eleven years Speer trekked from Berlin across Europe, through southern Asia, across China, over the Bering Strait, down through Canada along the west coast of America and into Mexico. With each lap around the garden, he walked himself into a kind of astral trance where his mind, now estranged from his body, was free to wander the earth.

The peripatetic prisoner carefully recorded in his diary the details of the places he had visited. '*July 13, 1959*: Arrived in Peking today. As I came to the Imperial Palace, some kind of demonstration was taking place in the great square outside it.' '*February 24, 1963*: In the immediate vicinity of Bering Strait, still craggy, hilly country, endless view of treeless rocky landscape.'

The world Speer traversed wasn't merely a blank landscape, but one animated by its own topographic narrative. 'Stories are compasses and architecture,' writes Rebecca Solnit. 'We navigate by them, we build our sanctuaries and our prisons out of them, and to be without a story is to be lost in the vastness of a world that spreads in all directions like arctic tundra or sea ice.'

Unburdened by the practicalities and discontentments of actual travel – cumbersome luggage, losing one's passport, waiting for flights, getting lost, tired, sunburnt and so on – Speer was free to experience the world exactly as he desired. It rained when he chose it to rain. The mountains were steep, if he felt so inclined. He got lost when it was convenient. Speer took armchair travel to an entirely new level. Like a solitary pilgrim, he journeyed across the boundless landscape of his own imagination, transcending not only the physical boundaries of the prison walls, but also the temporal and spatial boundaries of the world itself. On his last night in prison he sent a telegram to a friend that read, 'Please pick me up thirty-five kilometres south of Guadalajara, Mexico.'

By the time Speer stepped out of prison a free man on the stroke of midnight 1 October 1966, he had walked a total of 31,816 kilometres around the globe. Ironically, after prison he didn't travel at all. In fact, the *weltschmerz* traveller rarely left his Heidelberg villa. He did, however, take one final trip. On 1 September 1981, he flew to England for an interview with the BBC. After arriving in London, he checked into a hotel, collapsed on the floor, and died.

The enormous cement cylinder looked appropriately forbidding and vaguely extraterrestrial. I had Speer's diary in my bag but didn't take it out on account that someone might see it and think I was one of *those* people, one of those whose interest in Nazi architecture extends beyond healthy historical interest to disconcerting zealotry. The guide, a middle-aged woman with an angular German accent and a green, puffy winter coat, was repeating the name of the structure to a group of foreign tourists, of which I was one. '*Schwerbelastungskörper*,' she said, repeating the word slowly several times, but not slow enough for anyone to replicate the sounds convincingly.

'It simply means "heavy load-bearing body" in German.' She added a further note about the way Germans like to combine many words together into one single, very long and unpronounceable word. I left the group and tried to get a photograph of the structure, which stubbornly refused to fit into my camera frame.

'Because Berlin was built on soft swampy land, it was important to know the carrying capability of the underlying soil,' continued the guide. 'Hitler and Albert Speer's plans for the new city of World Capital Germania would require a lot of very heavy building materials. So, in 1941, Speer designed this structure as an experiment to test the strength of the ground. It is eighteen metres high and weighs roughly 12,650 tonnes. Because of the size and density of the structure, it is impossible to safely destroy.' This last comment led to some creative suggestions from various amateur demolition enthusiasts.

However abhorrent and visually unspectacular the *Schwerbelastungskörper* was, it was there to stay. Perhaps this indestructible object will be the last remaining ruin of a post-human city. Thinking of Nabokov, who said that, '…the future is but the obsolete in reverse,' I imagined the confusion it may pose to archaeologists of the distant future who will ponder endlessly over the structure as we do Stonehenge. I imagined them in white overalls, their tiny brushes sweeping away the layers of time, scouring the surface of the enigmatic artifact in search of clues to its forgotten function. But all they will find are the vestiges of colourful spray paint, those incomprehensible hieroglyphics dating from the early 21st century. Irrespective of the future, the object was now both an official landmark and unofficial memorial to the failed plans of World Capital Germania, an indestructible scar on the surface of a city pinned under the weight of its own history.

The gloomy pre-winter sky of Berlin was a solid grey mass, and the immense concrete structure appeared as if it were made from it. After taking a few more photos, I left and walked west towards the neighbourhood of Wilmersdorf.

I took out a scrap of paper, on which I had written the last Berlin address of Walter Benjamin. It is difficult to overstate the impact of Benjamin's work on contemporary society and culture. Whether writing about consumerism or French literature, smoking hash or Marxism, photography or Parisian shopping arcades, a philosophy of history or his childhood memories of Berlin, Benjamin's ideas and observations shimmer with an intensity of illumination that permeates almost every recess of modern life.

The oldest of three children, Benjamin was born in 1892 and grew up in an affluent Jewish household in the west Berlin suburb of Charlottenburg. His father was an auctioneer in antiques and art, while his mother owned a number of ice-skating rinks around the city. In 1902, when he was ten years old, Benjamin was enrolled in the Kaiser Friedrich School in Charlottenburg. He was a fragile and sickly child, so much so that in 1905 he was sent to a boarding school in the Thuringian countryside for two years, only returning to Berlin in 1907. This journey would mark the beginning of a lifetime of restless continental wandering for Benjamin. At the time of his death in 1940, he had no fewer than twenty-eight different addresses.

I walked down the empty cobbled streets of Ebers Strasse, darted through the oncoming traffic of Dominicus Strasse, along Fritz-Elsas-Strasse and into Rudolph-Wilde Park. The last time I had walked through this park was in the midst of a hot Berlin summer, but now the landscape was all but frozen, a scene of bleak decomposition, consisting of varying shades of brown and grey. At one end of the park a golden deer stands on a tall cement column in the centre of a dry fountain, its triumphant posture and opulent glow seeming to ridicule the organic decay of the autumn landscape around it. Submerged under fur coats and toting yappy dogs, a cluster of old women puffed white clouds into the cold air like a gathering of antique steam engines. I came out of the park, headed west along Waghäuseler Strasse, turned left onto Prinzregenten Strasse and easily found building number 66.

'You have to follow the author,' writes Benjamin in a review of Franz Hessel's 1929 book *On Foot in Berlin*, 'into the "Old West" of Berlin to get to know this side of him… how he celebrates the last monuments of an ancient culture of dwelling.' This neighbourhood was once home to some of Berlin's most prominent Jewish families. The apartment complex was pale yellow, the colour of seasickness, and composed of bare angular shapes, functional and inornate. Benjamin had his apartment on the fifth floor. It had a sunlit study with a generous view and enough room for his modest library of some 2,000 books. Just down the hall lived his cousin Egon Wissing and his wife Gert and often they would hang out together and smoke hash. He lived here until 1933, the year that Hitler became Chancellor of Germany. Shortly after that, life for German Jews became increasingly difficult. No longer able to support himself from his writing, and with attempts to write under pseudonyms such as K.A. Stampflinger and Detlef Holz proving fruitless, he sublet his apartment and left for Spain. Unknown to him at the time, he would not see Berlin again.

I stepped over a stout metal fence and walked around the side of the building. A small rectangular plaque attached to the wall read: 'BERLIN COMMEMORATIVE PLAQUE. From 1930 until his emigration in 1933 in the house which previously stood here lived WALTER BENJAMIN literary critic, essayist and philosopher.'

I was taken aback by the words, 'in the house which previously stood here'. This wasn't even the same building? It shouldn't have mattered but somehow it did. It was not enough simply for the address to be the same; I wanted the building to be the same, the same bricks and mortar, the same gate, the same windows and stairs. But what difference should it make? And yet, it did make a difference. My disappointment was there, in all its glorious undeniability. I walked back out onto the empty street and reluctantly took several photos of the building that Benjamin didn't once live in. From a window on the third floor, a pale wrinkled face glared down through floral curtains. It was a hollow, haunting face, with dark, deep-set eyes. Those were eyes, I thought to myself, that had seen things. Surely vexed at the sight of Benjamin pilgrims coming and going, leaving nothing and failing to contribute to the local economy, it was a look of dismay, of mild suspicion and bemusement. After all, wasn't it the very same look that I myself had given to the crippled pilgrims in Lourdes, France – a look that said, 'You do realize that's just ordinary water, don't you?' Yet, undeniable is the ancient human desire to travel to places of religious, spiritual or otherwise imagined significance, to drink from the spring, kiss the wall, touch the soil, read a plaque, take a photograph.

I found a U-Bahn entrance and jogged down the steps into the dimly lit burrow, leaping onto a train just as the doors were closing. On the seat next to me lay a folded newspaper. An aerial photograph of blue sea stretched across the front page. I leaned a little closer to see that the water was filled with bodies, some in fluorescent life jackets, floating and drifting around the up-turned hull of a small boat.

I got off at Wilmersdorfer Strasse and walked a few minutes to a large open-plan piazza. It was rectangular shaped; on either side ran identical, newly built dark grey buildings, propped up by cement colonnades. At the far end of the grey-tiled piazza, icy water blasted from holes in the ground into the listless afternoon air. The piazza was mostly empty, apart from a few solitary business people traversing from one end to the other. I had arrived at Walter-Benjamin-Platz. I strolled slowly from one end to the other, then back again. There was no denying it, the piazza – Benjamin's piazza – was an incredibly dull and azoic place. Its architects had designed it with flawless symmetry, yet the effect was not one of balanced refinement, but instead turned one's own body into a flawed glitch, a disruption in the absolute order and high-strung frequency of the space. In essence, there was nothing about Walter-Benjamin-Platz which resonated as having any kinship to Walter Benjamin the person. I came to think of the arbitrary nature of place names; that only too often the relationship between place and name is ill-considered or simply non-existent. I found a café just off the square, took a seat and, in my best German, ordered a sandwich and coffee.

It was just a few kilometres west of where I was that in 1933, the year Benjamin left Berlin, Reichskanzler Platz was renamed Adolf-Hitler-Platz. In Gdynia, Poland, Świętojańska Street became Adolf-Hitler-Strasse. In Rome, Italy, Viale dei Partigiani became Viale Adolf Hitler. Across all of Europe, from Holland to Russia, streets, parks, squares, bridges and stadiums were being renamed after *Der Führer*. These were no longer neutral public places, but politically charged spaces. However, by the end of the war in 1945, places named after Hitler had understandably grown out of fashion. They now served as reminders of death, destruction and shame. Original place names were either restored or new ones were given. In East Germany, the Soviets wasted little time in utilizing the political, ideological and pedagogical potential of place names. Streets were given names such as Karl-Marx-Allee, Stalinallee, Leninallee, Ernst Thälmann Strasse, Rosa Luxemburg Strasse. While we use place names to navigate the world, to mark, refer to and identify one place from another, there is also an unintended effect: they simultaneously laminate and amplify one's experience of that space.

This process of naming and renaming accentuates the fluidity of history. It suggests that history is not fixed but palimpsestic, an unceasing erasure and rewriting of the past from the shifting perspectives of the present and future. History is an unstable landscape made not from stone but sand, existing for a moment before the incoming tide of the future rewrites the past.

Much of the renaming that took place in unified Germany after the 1990s had not a political, but commemorative function. Streets and places were frequently renamed after individuals and Jewish communities that had been murdered at the hands of the Nazis. As a result, a number of Berlin's street names now read like

A street being renamed Adolf Hitler Strasse in 1939 in former Klaipeda Region, now Lithuania. Getty Images.

ghost stories. They recall the memory of the nameless; a subtle reminder for those in the present of the absence that haunts them from the past. It is through names, Benjamin suggests, that we discover connections that have the potential to transform an accepted history of that place, to reveal other cities within a city.

It is through street names, writes Benjamin, that, '...the city is image of a linguistic cosmos'.

I had arranged to meet my friend at a bar in Neukölln later that afternoon, so I decided to spend the next few hours walking there. It wasn't long, however, before I was thoroughly disorientated in the residential neighbourhood of Schöneberg. Perhaps nothing defines Berlin more for me than the sense of forest-like quietness and mountain spaciousness so rarely found in cities. Even in the middle of the day, one can find themselves completely alone on a Berlin street. It's hardly surprising; the city's population is smaller now than it was in 1925.

I wandered down the middle of the empty streets, attuned to the silence, peering up at the buildings that on either side formed walls like an ancient canyon.

'Not to find one's way around a city does not mean much,' writes Benjamin in his memoir *Berlin Childhood Around 1900.* 'But to lose one's way in a city, as one loses one's way in a forest, requires some schooling. Street names must speak to the urban wanderer like the snapping of dry twigs, and little streets in the heart of the city must reflect the times of day, for him, as clearly as a mountain valley.'

It began to rain, hard bullet drops, possibly infused with ice. I looked for cover and saw the fluorescent lights of a small convenience store across the street. I jogged over and stepped into the brightly lit room. The store was virtually empty save for a row of shelves on which sat a selection of canned goods, appearing more like museum relics than potential foodstuff. Several plastic buckets of dried bananas and apricots, also dating from a historical period beyond living memory, sat on the floor. In one corner of the store a group of Arabic men stood around a small plastic television bolted to the wall. I took a can of warm Coke from a non-functioning fridge and placed it loudly on the glass counter. They were watching silent news footage of what appeared to be a refugee camp on fire. A stream of despondent men were walking past the camera, some towing expensive-looking black suitcases behind them, as if casually heading for the airport departure gate. In the distance, makeshift tents blazed furiously. For a moment, the screen went hazy and one of the men slapped it several times with an open palm, jolting the image back into focus. The camera was now zoomed in on a single column of smoke as it drifted skywards. It followed the churning ebony and grey form as it ambled into the glass-blue stratosphere, monitoring its elopement from material captivity. I put the correct amount of change on the glass counter and left the store. Outside, the rain had stopped and the streets glistened as if freshly glazed.

Unable to return to Berlin, Benjamin once again went back to Paris, where he rented a small apartment at 10 Rue Dombasle. Supported by stipends, he resumed work on his critical study of Baudelaire and began what he hoped would be his magnum opus: the *Arcades Project*. As the name suggests, its focus was centred on the glass-roofed shopping arcades of 19th century Paris, taking the form of a montage of fragmented notes and quotations, arranged in thirty-six categories under titles such as 'Idleness', 'Mirrors', 'Dreams of the Future', 'Photography', 'The Collector', 'Advertising' and 'Prostitution'.

It was now 1940. Germany's invasion of the east cast an ominous shadow over the rest of Europe. While Benjamin felt reasonably safe in his Paris apartment, the strain and indigence of seven years in exile was taking its toll. He slumped into depression, avoiding even his closest friends, and rarely left his apartment. He struggled to continue work on his study of Baudelaire and the *Arcades Project*. He tried, with little hope, to apply for French citizenship, 'circumspectly,' he writes, 'but without illusions'. He was saddened by the situation of the Jews in Germany, his inability to find work, his sister's prognosis of disease, the loss of his work and belongings left behind in his Berlin apartment, which, he supposed, was now in the hands of the Gestapo. 'One realises,' he wrote, 'that the air is hardly fit to breathe any more – a condition of course which loses all significance as one is being strangled.' Benjamin grew increasingly desperate, writing to friends to send him money and tobacco. He tried harder than ever to find a way to America. To be able to afford a ticket, he attempted to sell his most cherished possession – Paul Klee's painting *Angelus Novus* – but failed to find a buyer.

In early May of 1940, German armies invaded Belgium and the Netherlands. Then, to Benjamin's horror, they breached the French border on 10 May and surged towards Paris. A wave of more than two million refugees was now streaming before the invading Nazi armies. In a panic, Benjamin collected his belongings, packing his most valuable work along with some clothes, a few toiletries, a gas mask and a single book into a suitcase. With his sister Dora, he jumped on one of the last trains leaving Paris for the small Pyrenean town of Lourdes, near the Spanish border. The very next day the German army entered Paris. A group of soldiers arrived at Benjamin's apartment and broke down the door, only to find an empty room.

I eventually stumbled across a U-Bahn station, which in Berlin never seem to be far from anywhere, and got off at U Rathaus Neukölln. I climbed the steps to Karl-Marx-Strasse and was met with an intensity of noise and activity that was a jolt to my senses. Following directions that my friend had texted me, I walked into a shopping mall and took the elevator to the roof. The bar was perched on top of the shopping centre and provided spectacular views over the city. I bought a beer and returned outside to the cool afternoon air. The sun now lingered on the horizon, illuminating parts of the city in golden columns of light.

Shortly after Benjamin and Dora arrived in Lourdes, the French authorities closed the border to Spain, forbidding all foreign nationals to travel without a permit.

'I cannot conceal from myself the peril of this situation,' wrote Benjamin. 'I fear that only a few will be able to save themselves.' After more than two torturous months of waiting in Lourdes, Benjamin learned he had secured a visa for America and that he should travel to the consulate in Marseilles. In early August, Benjamin and Dora arrived there to discover a city flooded with refugees, all desperate to flee war-torn Europe. Dora arranged a hiding place for herself on a country farm, and said a tearful farewell to her brother – they would never see each other again.

Along with his visa for America, Benjamin received transit visas for both Spain and Portugal, but most frustratingly, what he could not get was an exit visa from France. In late September, Benjamin and two friends took a train from Marseilles to the town

Benjamin's passport photograph from 1928. Image courtesy of the Walter Benjamin Archiv, Berlin.

of Port-Vendres, near the Spanish border. With the possibility of a simple and legal exit from France now impossible, the three friends decided to attempt a secret border crossing into Spain. From there, Benjamin could make his way to Portugal and onto a steamship for America. In Port-Vendres they joined Lisa Fittko, the wife of a man Benjamin knew. She was familiar with the area and knew of a little-used path that went over the Pyrenees mountains, across the French border and into the Spanish town of Portbou.

On 25 September, the group began their trek over the mountains, all the while terrified of being captured by the French police or border guards. With his ill health, Benjamin struggled to keep up. The late September days were hot and the mountains steep. For the entire journey since leaving Paris, he had carried a heavy black leather attaché case, which he stubbornly refused to let anyone else carry. It contained his new manuscript. 'This briefcase is most important to me,' Benjamin said to Fittko. 'The manuscript must be saved. It is more important than I am, more important than myself.'

On 26 September, the group crossed the Spanish border and that afternoon strolled into Portbou. Elated that they had escaped France, they located the customs office to get stamps for transit across Spain. But their elation was short-lived: they were informed that the border was closed and they would be returned to France the following day. It is difficult to imagine the depth of despair they must have felt as they were escorted to a small hotel, the Fonda de Francia, where they were kept under guard for the night. Exhausted and devastated, Benjamin couldn't bear the thought of being returned to France, where he would most certainly be interned and sent to a concentration camp, and perhaps worst of all, his manuscript would be handed over to the Gestapo. He lay on his hotel bed, a large golden watch on the table next to him and his attaché case by his side.

In the morning, the group awoke to find Benjamin dead in his hotel room. He had swallowed several handfuls of morphine pills the night before. The next day the border was reopened. The group was not returned to France. They left Benjamin's body, continued on to Lisbon and, eventually, America.

Hannah Arendt came to Portbou several months later, but she could not find Benjamin's grave. She found, however, a document recorded at the time of Benjamin's death listing his personal belongings: a pocket watch and chain, a 500-franc bill, a fifty-dollar bill, a twenty-dollar bill, a passport with a Spanish visa and American visa, six photographs, an ID card, an X-ray, a wooden pipe, a pair of glasses, and several letters and newspapers. But no body and no manuscript. The manuscript, which Benjamin considered more important than himself, had disappeared completely and to this day has not been found. Some believe it was the *Arcades Project* in its final form, or perhaps something else entirely.

As I waited for my friend to arrive at the bar, I wondered what Benjamin was thinking as he lay in his hotel bed that September night, the morphine softly tugging at his consciousness, carrying it towards the darkness of eternal night. Perhaps he thought of Berlin, the quiet cobbled streets of Charlottenburg, the dark musty rooms of his childhood home. It is not life but death that Benjamin believed to be the source of both the story and the storyteller. 'Just as a sequence of images is set in motion inside a man as his life comes to an end…death is the sanction of everything that the storyteller can tell. He has borrowed his authority from death. In other words, it is natural history to which his stories refer back.'

In German, the word *Geschichte* means both story and history. This double meaning suggests that history is a kind of story, and a story a kind of history. While we associate stories with the imaginary and history with facts, perhaps they are instead one and the same, merging into each other the way a freshwater stream flows into the sea. The history of the place, that is, the story of place, is, in the words of Benjamin, a story, '…revealed through the layers of a variety of retellings'.

I leaned against the railing and looked north across the city. The sky had now shed its grey coat and the light of a few stars, or the spectral glow of dead stars, penetrated the dull haze. The first street lights were now coming on.

Benjamin had been fascinated by a very Borgesian idea formed during the French Revolution of, '…transforming Paris into a map of the world: all streets and squares were to be rechristened and their new names drawn from noteworthy places and things across the world'. He also notes Louis-Sébastien Mercier, who on a more modest scale suggested that Parisian street names should be renamed after French towns and landscapes, '…taking into consideration their geographical position relative to each other,' noting that the size of the town should reflect the size of the street. French rivers and mountains would be represented by particularly long streets that span across several districts, '… to provide an ensemble such that a traveller could acquire geographic knowledge of France within Paris, and reciprocally, of Paris within France'. Benjamin quotes J.B. Pujoulx, who writes what a pleasure it would be, '…for the resident of the South of France to rediscover, in the names of the various districts of Paris, those of the place where he was born, of the town where his wife came into the world, of the village where he spent his early years'.

This overlapping and interweaving of spatialities led my thoughts once more to Speer's imaginary wanderings. Perhaps the world is simultaneously both internal and external, an entire cosmos contained within a city, the world within a garden, the story of a place in a name, and to experience it, perhaps we need go no further than the threshold of our own mind. Looking over the city, I once more felt certain that this historical construction, this arrangement of temporal and spatial realities in which I now stood, was merely an arbitrary outcome of an unlimited set of futures, a story in which the layering of realities lay folded before and behind me like a book with no beginning or end. It felt, as it were, as if I were living the memory of a nameless future.

In Portbou there is a memorial to Benjamin designed by Israeli artist Dani Karavan titled *Passages*. It's a long, rusted steel corridor that descends down weather-worn steps to the glistening sea below. But at the end, before one can reach the sea, the steps are met with an impenetrable glass wall.

Six years after Speer died in a London hotel, Spandau prison was demolished. A shopping mall was rapidly built on the site of the prison and Speer's garden was paved over with cement and turned into a parking lot. To be certain that not a trace of the prison remained from which a potential memorial site could be formed, the entire building was pulverized into a fine powder and dumped into the sea.

Dani Karavan's memorial to Walter Benjamin in Portbou, Spain, titled *Passages*.
Image courtesy of Nicolas Veyssiere.

• 54°52'8.21"N
• 1°41'55.83"W

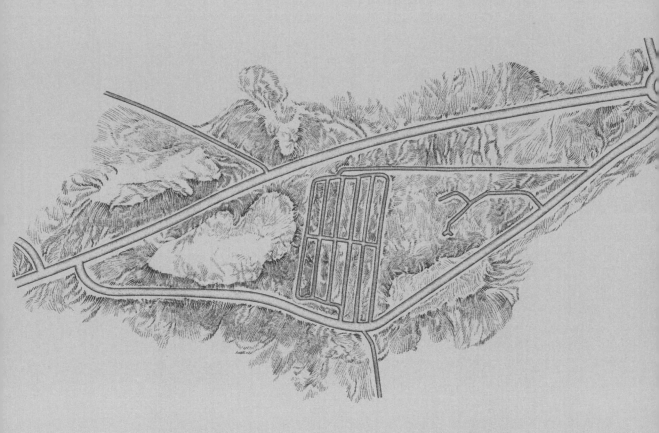

No Place

No Place, Durham, England

IF YOU STUMBLE across No Place, you will likely be disappointed to find it has no cinema, no 7-Eleven, no gas station, no train station, no shopping mall and not even a town sign. Perhaps it is this last absence that is its greatest missed opportunity. 'There's No Place like home', the sign could dryly exclaim. Or perhaps, 'There's no place like No Place'.

Yet, No Place is not the negative spatial construct that its name suggests. Located in north-east England, in a sparsely inhabited landscape of rolling hills and endless motorways, soot-coloured clouds and furniture hypermarkets, No Place can be easily missed. Consisting simply of six identical streets, the town forms a grid of twelve rows of red-brick, two-storey terraced houses in which some 300 inhabitants dwell in placeless resignation.

No Place began its nondescript and tenuous existence around the end of the 19th century as a cluster of four terraced houses, compressed on either end by two large housing estates. The story, as told by the locals, recounts that the name 'no place' was given to the houses because they failed to qualify as a legitimate town. Nevertheless, as the decades passed, the non-town slowly expanded out of its own placelessness. During the town's brief heyday of the 1950s the town boasted a Co-op, fish and chip shop, bakery, corner store and even a dedicated sweet shop. Most of the expanding town's residents worked at the nearby Beamish Mary coal pit. They lived half of their lives in No Place and the other half in a mine, and since the act of mining is that of creating negative space, the inhabitants brought a kind of poetic circularity to No Place.

Life progressed with the usual lacklustre pace of such English villages until, in the late 1950s, Durham County Council quietly decided to commit No Place to slow extinction. It wasn't so much a course of action as a plan of non-action. As the town's population had been in slow decline over the years, and as the town's upkeep posed a considerable financial burden to the county, planners decided they would neither repair buildings nor invest in new housing and infrastructure. Eventually, it was reasoned, the town would meet its destiny.

In a sense, albeit less dramatic, they were attempting to condemn it to *damnatio memoriae*; the Latin term meaning 'condemnation of memory' was an ancient form of punishment handed down by the Roman Senate to traitors or those who had dishonoured the empire. To be condemned was to be made a non-person. It was forbidden to acknowledge, speak or write the name of the condemned and every physical trace of their life in Rome was destroyed. After their death, it would be as if they had never existed. To be erased from the memory of the future was considered, by many, as the most severe form of punishment. For both people and cities, death may be an inevitable consequence of life, but there is a certain compensation, or redemptive quality, in the immortality of memory. In a 1953 interview with *Time* magazine, the local church minister said, 'Some think No Place is doomed because of its name. But to the villagers it is home and there is no place like it.' (The pun was surely intended.) French theorist Marc Augé coined the term *non-place* to describe places of transience. Airports, hotel rooms and shopping centres are not destinations, Augé argues, but transitional spaces for passage and consumption. This, however, is entirely subjective. A highway underpass is neither a home nor destination; unless you're the vagabond living there. Despite its name, and everything it lacked, the residents of No Place had made it a place. Under the threat of extinction, the town united and resisted, fighting and winning against the county council.

Thirty years later, in 1983, the county again attempted to meddle in the town's affairs. With undoubtedly the best intentions in mind, they wanted to give No Place a name. The proposed title of 'Co-operative Villas', the county believed, would finally solidify its transient identity. What they failed to understand, however, was that No Place was al-

The Severan Tondo, a circa AD 199 panel painting of the Severan family. The portrait of Geta's face has been erased because of the *damnatio memoriae* ordered by his brother.

ready their identity, it was the name of their home. To change the town's name was to erase its past, a past that the town had fought so hard to keep. If the first attempt to erase No Name had been physical, then this one was metaphysical. But, once again, the town rejected the identity change (actually, it was more of a compromise – road signs now read both 'Co-operative Villas' and 'No Place'). It may be a town defined by negatives, but it nevertheless has a lot of positives. There is a chapel, pub and football field, and, perhaps most importantly, an almost endless supply of bad puns.

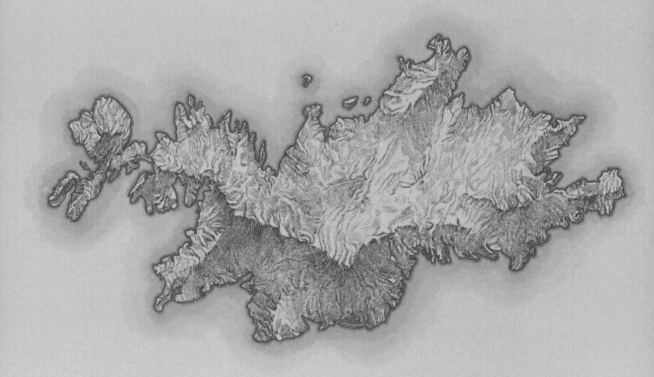

• 50°36.25 S
 • 165°58.38 E

Disappointment Island

Disappointment Island,

Auckland Islands, New Zealand

6 *MARCH 1907. FIFTEEN* men huddled together on a barren outcrop of rocks in the southern Pacific Ocean. A frigid Antarctic gale howled around their wet, quivering bodies. Through the impenetrable darkness came the roar of the ocean, furiously pulverizing their wooden ship against the island's cliffs. For the shipwrecked men, this unmistakable sound came to epitomize their predicament. It was the sound of disappointment.

They had arrived on Disappointment Island. While it's unknown who christened it, it is a name that would prove particularly apt. While one's ordinary life may offer select moments of disappointment: a poorly chosen birthday gift, the lack of chicken in a chicken Caesar salad, rain during a Sunday picnic – on Disappointment Island, as if by prophecy, *everything* was disappointing. If

it were not enough to be shipwrecked with next to no hope of rescue, there were plenty of other reasons to be disappointed. To begin with, unlike other, more fortunate nautical castaways in the tropics who were stranded on glistening white sands and palm tree paradises, the castaways on Disappointment Island were met with an infinitesimal mound of brittle windswept rock. It was not glassy, turquoise waters that surrounded it, but the dark, storm-ravaged Southern Ocean. One man, '…after finding he was not on the main Auckland Island' but on Disappointment Island, was overwhelmed with such disappointment that he, '…died on the twelfth day after the wreck', possibly making him the only person in history to succumb to death from disappointment.

Seventeen days earlier, on 17 February 1907, the castaways' ship, the *Dundonald* – a 220-foot, steel-hulled vessel – pulled out of Sydney Harbour laden with wheat and bound for England. The journey east that was to take them around Cape Horn had been going smoothly until they were caught in a wild squall, a common event at the longitude universally known to sailors as the Roaring Forties. Their plans to ride it out were thwarted when, just after midnight, they saw land and, unable to manoeuvre the cumbersome vessel in time, were impelled into the island's malicious cliffs. The ship heaved violently against the rocks and men frantically scrambled in the chaos of darkness. Wave after wave swept over the deck, hurling them into the churning ocean. Those fortunate enough to escape the sinking ship desperately clambered up the island's 300-foot stone cliffs. Sixteen of the twenty-eight men had made it ashore alive. One man had reached the safety of land only to be clawed back in by a vengeful wave. He was never seen again. After the unfathomable ordeal, when the morning sun finally illuminated their pale, frozen bodies, the men stood and gazed around at the barren rock on which they found themselves. Their spirits, briefly raised at having survived, were quickly dashed – the island was a truly disappointing sight.

In the following days, the men took turns venturing out to the shipwreck, tearing canvas from the mast that only just peeked above the ocean's surface. Starving, the men caught mollyhawks and devoured their raw flesh. In the last moments before abandoning ship, one of the men had grabbed several matches, but they were sodden from the sea. It took three days before the matches had dried enough to start a fire – one that they could never allow to go out.

The men had little choice but to be industrious. Their makeshift canvas tent proved no match for the raging winter snowstorms, and as there was no timber on the island, they burrowed holes with their bare hands into the frozen ground and fashioned shelters from shrubs and sticks. They crafted slippers from seal fur. They tailored blankets and clothing from salvaged sail canvas, stitched together with grass fibre and bone needles. They built clay ovens and baked every creature they encountered: mollyhawks, albatrosses, mutton birds, whale birds and, on occasion, the unsuspecting sea lion. One can only imagine the unbearable torment of knowing that, before their unscheduled stay on Disappointment Island, they were riding on thousands of tons of golden wheat, enough to happily feed each man many lifetimes over. Days dragged into weeks and weeks into months. Each day, the men gazed with hollow disappointment across the vast and empty horizon. In desperation, they attached rescue messages to the legs of albatrosses.

Only eight kilometres to the east of Disappointment Island lay Auckland Island. While also uninhabited, it was significantly larger and, more importantly, was rumoured to house an emergency food storage. The obvious difficulty was how to reach it without a boat. As history has repeatedly shown, there is nothing like moments of great desperation to inspire feats of great ingenuity. From sail canvas and the wiry branches of the *Veronica elliptica* plant, they lashed together a small boat that resembled an enormous floating basket. From sticks and canvas they built makeshift oars. Then, three men climbed into their fragile creation and with a wave and a cheer, they set off to the neighbouring island. However, their success in making it to the island was dampened by their inability to locate the elusive supplies. Then, as if by a curse whereby they were doomed to repeat their earlier misfortune, their delicate craft was shattered against the rocks as they returned, empty-handed and dejected, to Disappointment Island.

Survivors onboard the *Hinemoa* together with their handmade craft which they used to escape Disappointment Island.

But by early October they had built another bigger boat and this time four men set off once more. They made it to Auckland Island, but their boat was again crushed as they met the rocks. On the fourth day, after an agonizing 20-kilometre trek to the other side of Auckland Island through thicket and scrub that tore at their skin, they stumbled across the elusive food store and, much to their delight, a small wooden rowboat. After cutting up their clothes to make sails, the men, naked yet triumphant, journeyed back to Disappointment Island to collect their stranded friends – together returning to their new larger and much less disappointing island.

The castaways erected a patchwork flag on which they wrote not 'Help!' or 'SOS', but 'Welcome'. It must have worked because shortly after, on 16 October, the New Zealand government steamer *Hinemoa* was passing by on a Subantarctic Islands scientific expedition when, by sheer chance, they noticed the flag flying at half-mast – the universal sign of a shipwrecked crew. After anchoring and discovering the weary survivors, *Hinemoa*'s captain announced, with much anticlimactic disappointment, that they could not be rescued until the science expedition was complete, until which time they must continue to wait patiently on Auckland Island. The men, who had suffered so much disappointment, resigned themselves to yet a little more.

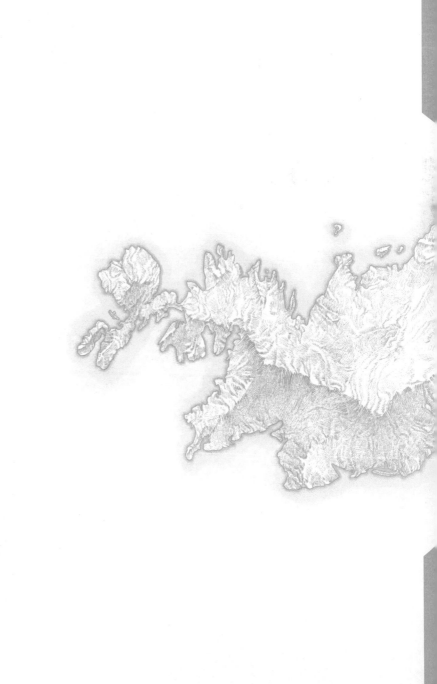

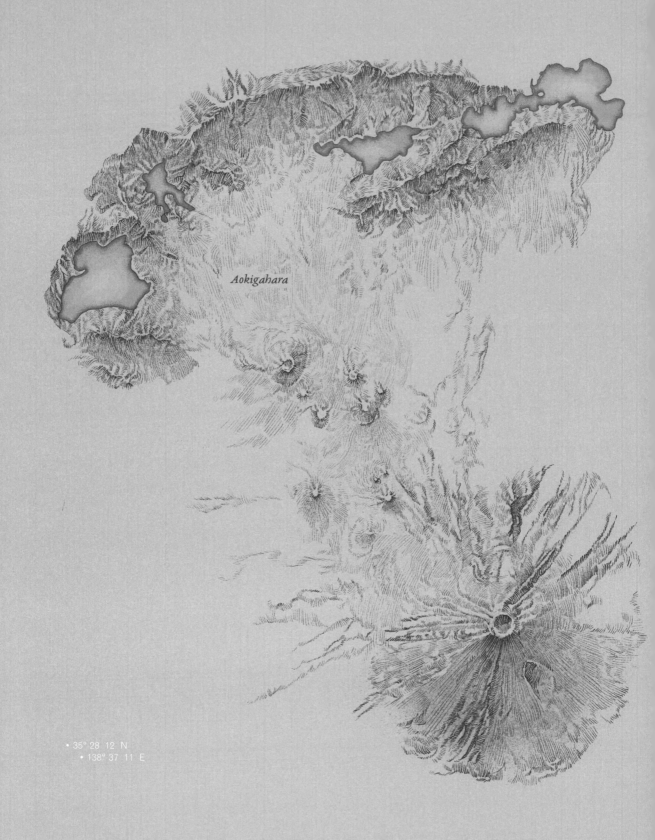

Aokigahara

• 35° 28 12 N
  • 138° 37 11 E

Suicide Forest (Aokigahara), Japan

THE COMPLETE MANUAL *of Suicide* called it the perfect place to die. In the year 864, the sixth year of the Jōgan era, Mount Fuji erupted for ten days straight. An enormous river of lava flowed from its flaming maw and ash rained down from the sky to form a fiery blanket over the land, one that stretched from the volcano to the sea. The landscape instantly ignited, engulfing forests and entire villages in a scene of apocalyptic destruction. Over the next 1,200 years, a dense interwoven forest of hemlock, cypress, red pine, conifer and Japanese oak grew from the rich volcanic soil. The forest that emerged was given the name 'Aokigahara'. Today, it forms an almost impenetrable wall of greenery. A tangled mass of roots, vines and interlocking foliage shrouds an undulating, moss-carpeted landscape of lava tubes and caves. Standing on the side of Mount Fuji and looking down on the forest, one can see nothing but a rolling ocean of chlorophyll, a sight for which Aokigahara also earned the name: The Sea of Trees.

Few modern cultures are as firmly steeped in myth and superstition as the Japanese. Its enduring mythologies and ritualistic practices have been transmitted over countless generations to form the foundations of contemporary Japanese society. Aokigahara acts as a bridge spanning the vast chasm of time and belief, a force uniting ancient spiritualism and modern Japanese culture. Yet, there is a sinister side to the forest. As one ancient myth has it, Aokigahara was used as a site for the highly questionable practice of *ubasute*. Meaning to 'abandon an old woman', it refers to the morbid act of carrying one's unwanted infirm family member or elderly relative into a forest where, through starvation and exposure, they are left die. Said to have been common practice during hard times of drought and famine, it was, as myth has it, even mandated by feudal officials. Myth also has it that the incremental accumulation of death and suffering experienced by those condemned to die alone in Aokigahara forest, combined with the misery of hundreds of individuals who wandered, albeit by their own accord, into its depths to die, has permeated the landscape with such potency as to puncture the boundaries of reality itself. It is said that, as a result, those who now wander in the forest, regardless of their intentions, are unable to leave.

Wanderers are not, by some accounts, the only occupants of the forest. Ghosts of the tormented are said to reside there as well. In Japanese, the word for ghost is *yūrei*, and much like their Western equivalents, they are believed to be the souls of those who have failed to successfully transition to the afterlife. Yet, unlike Western culture, there are many kinds of ghosts in Japanese mythology. Typically, *yūrei* are depicted as having long, black, dishevelled hair and wearing the clothes that they died in. *Yūrei*,

Depiction of *ubasute. The moon and the abandoned old woman*, Tsukioka Yoshitoshi (1867).
Art Gallery of New South Wales.

being the fastidious ghosts they are, have a preferred haunting time between 2 and 2.30 in the morning, when it is said that the membrane separating the world of the living from that of the dead is at its most fragile.

Aokigahara forest had been a popular suicide destination for hundreds of years, yet it wasn't until the 1960s, after the publi-cation of the novel *The Sea of Trees* by Seichō Matsumoto, that its popularity soared. The best-selling novel tells the story of a woman and her doomed love affair with a young man. When the young man is blackmailed by the woman's husband, in a dramatic Romeo and Juliet-style twist, the lovers flee to Aoki-gahara to end their lives in a suicide pact.

Aokigahara forest is emblematic of a larger cultural phenomenon in Japan, a country that has one of the highest suicide rates in the developed world. On average, there are some seventy suicides every day in Japan and, for at least a decade, the suicide rate has exceeded 30,000 a year. The 1997 stock market crash saw the suicide rate jump by 35 per cent. Japan is a country in which a mentality of self-sacrifice runs deep, where the act of taking one's life is not burdened by the same Judaeo-Christian connotation of sin as in the West. It is a culture not of individuality, but collectivity, with one person's embarrassment or failures resonating throughout the whole community. Unlike in the West, failure is not seen as a necessary obstacle on the path to success, but as a mark of shame from which there can be no recovery. In Japan, there is a culturally inherited and approved idea of honourable suicide, known as *seppuku*. The ritual – which involves slicing open or stabbing one's own stomach with a knife, undoubtedly resulting in a slow and agonizing death – was traditionally practised by the Samurai, and was considered a justified response to failure, a last-resort act in the face of defeat or capture. The notion of honourable suicide or self-sacrifice was further romanticized as a noble and patriotic deed by kamikaze pilots during the Second World War. These forerunners of suicide bombers believed that to sacrifice one's life for the Japanese Empire was the greatest deed of patriotism one could perform.

Aokigahara has earned itself the poignant distinction of being the world's second most popular suicide destination (second only to San Francisco's Golden Gate Bridge) and now goes by the more morbid epithet: Suicide Forest.

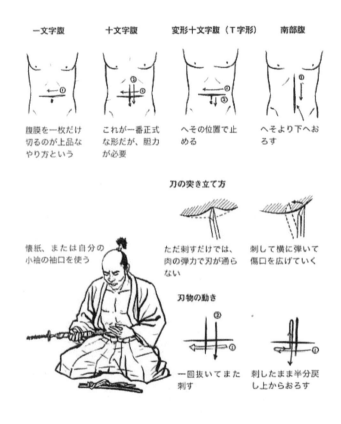

Tips for a successful *seppuku*.

Abandoned cars litter the visitor parking lot. Throughout the forest, wooden signs nailed to trees deliver messages such as: 'Your life is a precious gift from your parents!' and 'Please consult the police before you decide to die!' Over the years, it has been estimated that no fewer than 500 people have taken one-way hikes into the forest. A line of volunteers and park rangers scour the forest annually, searching for the remains of bodies. On one such hunt, a park ranger discovered a weathered skeleton slumped, almost reclined, against the base of a giant oak tree. The bones, which had assumed the hue of old snow, appeared like ancient fossils. A faded grey business suit clung to the emaciated form and the black leather shoes that pointed skywards now appeared oversized on the thin bones that projected into them. Around the skeleton, partially submerged in leaf matter, lay a scattering of various objects: a cell phone, black-framed glasses, a plastic water bottle and the faded pages of *The Complete Manual of Suicide* by Wataru Tsurumi, which still lay open, swollen by the rain. Here, these objects appeared like the ancient relics of some long-forgotten civilization. A slow tide of moss and vines, indifferent to the quiet horror of the scene, had begun consuming, reclaiming.

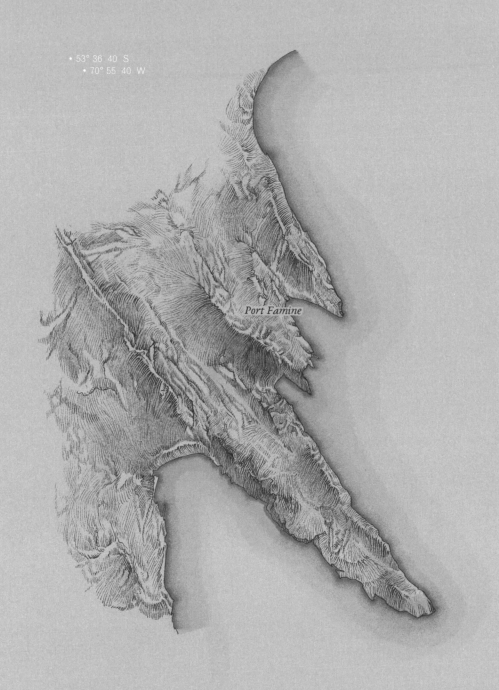

53° 36 40 S
70° 55 40 W

Port Famine

Port Famine, Patagonia, Chile

ON 11 FEBRUARY 1584, four ships arrived in the Strait of Magellan in southern Chile. Blistering gales roared up off the Antarctic ice sheet, now less than 700 miles south, and buffeted the ships as they attempted to set anchor offshore. Eventually, the 337 bewildered men, women and children of the ship's crew disembarked. After months of treacherous seafaring, their final destination was more desolate and inhospitable than any of them could have imagined. The destitute crew staggered over the frozen, windswept beach, towing behind them an enormous wooden cross. This land, declared Captain Sarmiento, was for the Spanish Empire. Here they will build a great city. It will be called *Ciudad del Rey Don Felipe* – 'City of King Philip'.

At the time, the Spanish Empire – intoxicated with plundered wealth and an overzealous enthusiasm for Christianity – was stretching far beyond the reaches of Europe. An abundance of silver, acquired through its so-called 'missionary' adventures in the Americas, had helped fund its expanding empire, as did the endless quantity of slave labour supplied by the natives themselves. The natives of the New World had initially greeted the first Spanish conquerors with open-armed hospitality, while the Spanish repaid their hosts with smallpox, supreme violence and slavery. 'The Indians,' writes Alain De Botton in *The Consolations of Philosophy*, 'were undermined by their own hospitality and by the weakness of their arms. They opened their villages and cities to the Spanish, to find their guests turning on them when they were least prepared. Their primitive weapons were no match for Spanish cannons and swords, and the *conquistadores* showed no mercy towards their victims. They killed children, slit open the bellies of pregnant women, gouged out eyes, roasted whole families alive and set fire to villages in the night.'

Three years earlier, on 27 September 1581, a fleet of twenty-three ships carrying 2,500 sailors, soldiers, priests and settlers, with their wives and children, left the Spanish port town of Cádiz destined for southern Chile. King Philip II had ordered the construction of a new city along the Strait of

Magellan, one that would protect their territory from rival colonialists. However, soon after leaving, the fleet experienced various calamities. Two ships were destroyed in a violent Atlantic storm, forcing the entire fleet to return to Spain. After two months they set sail again, but now with just sixteen ships and 2,200 men. The fleet continued to be plagued by storms and, by the time they reached the eastern entrance to the Strait of Magellan, only four ships remained – the rest had abandoned the mission and returned to Spain.

While most would see these ominous signs as portending more failure to come and simply call it a day, Capitan Sarmiento remained unfazed. With just four of the twenty-three ships, and 337 of the original 2,500 crew, he led the straggling remains of the fleet west along the Strait of Magellan, into the desolate and uncharted heart of Patagonia. Sarmiento, however, had no intention of sticking around. After just a few weeks, he boarded a ship back to Spain, leaving the bewildered settlers to build King Philip's city on their own.

OBSERVATOIRE DE PORT FAMINE

Observatoire de Port Famine, Dumont D'Urville (1848).

Of the settlers, there were two Franciscan priests, fifty-eight men, thirteen women, ten children and twenty-two tradesmen. The remainder were soldiers and sailors. The City of King Philip was far from the temperate climate and fertile lands of Spain. Seeds and crops were incapable of germinating in Patagonia's frigid conditions. The settlers had brought little more than naive hope, colonial arrogance and an enormous wooden cross to save them.

For nearly three years, nothing but inauspicious silence came from the City of King Philip. Sarmiento hadn't even made it back to Spain. A storm had forced his ship far out into the Atlantic Ocean where he and his crew ate the ship's cats and leather harnesses to survive. They eventually made it to Brazil, where Sarmiento sold his clothes to buy food. This, however, proved merely a brief reprieve from his misfortunes. While trying to return to Spain again, he was captured by the British pirate Walter Raleigh and then by the French, who kept him prisoner for almost three years in the gloomy castle of Mont-de-Marsan.

On 10 January 1587, the British navigator Thomas Cavendish was passing through the Strait of Magellan when he stopped at the City of King Philip to stock up on supplies. Onshore, he was met with a gruesome scene. Of the 337 settlers, only fifteen men and three women remained. Looking more like skeletons than humans, they precariously clung to the last vestiges of life. In the town's square, a decaying body swung from the gallows, a symbol of what had become of the city. Scattered among the ruins, Cavendish found the corpses of the city's frozen and starved population, prompting him to re-christen the city 'Port Famine'. Bizarrely, the gaunt survivors refused Cavendish's offer of rescue. Except for one man, that is – a sailor by the name of Tomé Hernández. At the port of Quintero, near Santiago, Hernández left the ship and went to the Governor of Chile to recount the City of King Philip's disastrous fate.

During the three years of silence, rumours abounded across Chile that the population of the City of King Philip had in fact abandoned their doomed city and stumbled across the 'City of the Caesars'. This mythical city, which also went by the name *Ciudad de los Césares*, the Wandering City and Trapalanda, was reportedly hidden in the Andes mountain range in Patagonia, somewhere between Chile and Argentina. The City of the Caesars, it was rumoured, appeared at only certain moments. The gold, silver and

Port Famine

diamonds from which it was built could be seen glistening from hundreds of miles away. Unfortunately, those who had discovered it, it was believed, were inconveniently struck by amnesia the moment they left.

Even years after the truth of the City of King Philip's gruesome fate had become widely known, rumours continued to persist. As W.H. Auden's poem 'Archaeology' goes: 'Knowledge may have its purposes, | but guessing is always | more fun than knowing.'

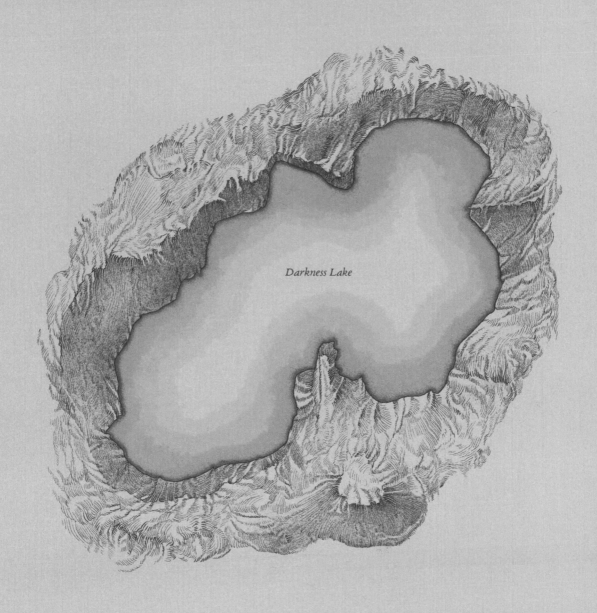

Darkness Lake

• 50°13'55" N
• 86°22'24" W

Darkness Lake, Ontario, Canada

HISTORICAL RECORDS REMAIN stubbornly silent on how a small lake, buried within the depths of the Canadian wilderness, came to be named Darkness. When one considers, however, the period during which the region was explored and mapped, and the curiously poetic names of neighbouring lakes, such as Poverty and Dusk, a possible story emerges. It's a story that has its beginnings in the summer of 1816, during what has become known as 'the summer of darkness'.

'We will each write a ghost story,' declared Lord Byron. The five friends huddled before the glowing fire of the Swiss villa. Although it was the middle of June, it could have easily been the middle of winter. Thunderstorms illuminated the sky and rain fell in biblical proportions. On the rare occasions when the rain ceased and the group ventured outside, they found the air suffused with an eerie red fog, so dense that the sun's rays created the effect of an endless dusk.

It was May, 1816. Lord Byron, who had fled England to escape both his pregnant wife and the controversy around his secret love affair with his half-sister, had decided to spend the summer in voluntary exile in a villa by Lake Geneva. For company, Byron had brought along his friend and personal physician John Polidori. In the villa opposite stayed the 18-year-old Mary Godwin with her lover Percy Shelley, their four-month-old son and Mary's stepsister, Claire Clairmont. They too had travelled from London to Lake Geneva for this summer vacation. More accurately, they had come at Claire Clairmont's insistence. After a brief fling in London, she had developed an infatuation for Byron that bordered on fanatic obsession. She was also secretly pregnant with his child. Together, the five young English bohemians hung out in Byron's villa – a strange but oddly suited bunch.

and rivers froze. Frosts and heavy rains destroyed crops in Ireland and England. Throughout mainland Europe, harvests failed and, in the face of starvation, people rioted and looted. It took more than two years for normality to return, but not before some 90,000 people across the globe had died, largely from starvation and disease.

Unsurprisingly, many believed that these unprecedented atmospheric events signified the end of the world. By sheer coincidence, an Italian astronomer from Bologna had predicted that on 18 July the sun would burn itself out and shroud the planet in eternal darkness. News of this dire prediction resulted in riots, suicides and a mass religious resurgence. The actual reason for the meteorological abnormality – unknown to everyone in Europe – was a volcanic eruption on 10 April 1815, the previous year. The eruption of Mount Tambora, in what is now Indonesia, was the most destructive volcanic event in recorded history – erupting with such explosive force that it instantly obliterated much of the mountain, generating a sound wave heard 1,600 miles away. Some 10,000 islanders were incinerated by tidal waves of pyroclastic flows. The eruption spewed billions of tons of ash, gas and debris into the atmosphere, which fell up to 800 miles away. For two days after the eruption, 350 miles surrounding the mountain were cast

As far as summer vacations go, it would have been ideal if not for the strangely unseasonal weather. The perpetual cold and darkness of that summer had been like none other in human memory. Unbeknown to the group, it extended even beyond Europe. In China, freezing temperatures killed trees, rice crops and animals. Snow fell across parts of North America. In Canada, lakes in complete darkness. The malicious cloud of ash, pumice and sulphur slowly crept around the world, taking a year to reach Europe and several months more to reach North America.

The disaster unfolding beyond Lake Geneva was, in terms of practical ramifications, a mere inconvenience to the group's Swiss summer vacation. The ordinarily glistening Lake Geneva now appeared sinister, mirroring the dark, thunderous sky. 'It proved a wet, ungenial summer,' wrote Mary, 'and incessant rain often confined us for days to the house.' The five friends cosied up around the warmth of the log fire, drinking French wine and talking politics and poetry into the early morning hours. In newspapers, they read about the mysterious weather and the apocalyptic hysteria taking hold of Europe. 'We continue to receive the most melancholy news from Germany on the extraordinary weather which afflicts nearly the whole of Europe,' wrote one French newspaper. 'The excessive abundance of rain has caused disasters almost everywhere.'

Etching of the 1815 eruption of Tambora in Indonesia.

As it happened, the disastrous summer also proved highly conducive to creativity that would permanently reshape the literary landscape. One evening, after reading from *Fantasmagoriana* – a collection of German horror stories – Byron proposed that everyone write their own; a kind of friendly literary contest. A few days later, Shelley produced *A Fragment of a Ghost Story*. Mary found inspiration in a nightmare in which she dreamt of a, '…pale student of unhallowed arts kneeling beside the thing he had put together'. It was a dream that she transformed into the beginnings of a story, one that would start at its end in a hostile world of ice and darkness. It would become one of the most influential works of modern literature: *Frankenstein; or, The Modern Prometheus*. John Polidori, meanwhile, produced a piece that he called *The Vampyre*. He would also publish it after returning to England, making it the first modern vampire novella. Byron had his own prophetic dream, 'which was not all a dream'. His contribution was a poem he named 'Darkness'. The poem is an ominous vision of the future, one preached by the apocalyptic prophets across Europe. The darkness of Byron's poem is not simply about an absence of light, but a bleak tale of the downfall of man into the abyss of darkness, the nihilistic condition of the human soul in the sun's absence. In 'Darkness', people are so desperate for warmth and light that they burn their houses and entire cities, the first act in their precipitous downfall into darkness. 'And men were gather'd round their blazing homes / To look once more into each other's face.' The darkness that had descended over the world permeates the hearts of men, robbing them of any vestige of their humanity. From the 'pang of famine', people 'fed upon all entrails' before turning on each other. The world becomes a, 'seasonless, herbless, treeless, manless, lifeless' rock suspended in the darkness of space. 'The rivers, lakes and ocean all stood still, And nothing stirr'd within their silent depths.'

The 1816 summer of darkness that inspired great works of literature also inspired Turner to paint his iconic, fiery-skied landscapes, Schubert's Symphony No. 4 (*Tragic*) and Beethoven's melancholy Piano Sonata No. 28. Oddly, it's even said to have inspired the invention of the first bicycle. Perhaps it was during that year of 'uncongenial weather' that one explorer came to name several lakes. And perhaps it was in one lake, one in which the dark sky of that summer was reflected, that the explorer saw and was moved by an unending darkness.

• 63° 0 0 N.
 • 23° 49 0 E

Kuolema

Death (Kuolema), Finland

DEATH IS A village in Finland. Near the centre of this Nordic country, in a flat, featureless landscape of tall pines and marshy fields, is the loose scattering of ten or so stout timber houses, some painted deep red and others arctic white. The village has no bank, church, pub or library. It lacks even a cemetery. A straight road divides the town in two, and one can drive through without even knowing it. Swedish photographer Eva Persson spent a year documenting the inhabitants of the village in a series titled *Elämää Kuolemassa,* or 'Life in Death'. 'Only in Finland can a village be called Death,' writes Persson. 'In Finland, you are born, then comes a long period of suffering, and then you die.' To understand Persson's comment, which at first may appear cruel or morbid, one must first understand that the Finnish identify with death and suffering like the British identify with tea and scones. Perhaps it is the country's unique geographical positioning (balancing between Eastern European pessimism and Scandinavian gloom) that gives rise to a species of melancholy particular to Finland. Yet Finnish melancholy embraces a humour as dark as the Arctic winters. 'When all hope is gone,' Finnish film director Aki Kaurismäki once dryly remarked in an interview, 'there is no reason for pessimism.'

Persson's photo series revolves around the lives of two identical twin sisters who run the village's only supermarket. In their conjoined house, located at the back of the supermarket, the sisters live together with their husbands who are themselves, incidentally, brothers. While the work was produced in 2002, it could have easily been 1982. In this Finnish village, mullets and moustaches thrive without irony and *The Bold and the Beautiful* features as the latest spectacle to arrive on prime-time television. If the function of death is to relieve the world of that which is redundant, then it appears that death has passed Death by.

There are several theories as to how the town earned its name. One rumour suggests that it occurred in 1888 when a motel innkeeper was murdered by a passing stranger; or, more likely, it originates from an old Finnish children's rhyme that goes *Halla, nälkä, kuolema; niskat nurin ja taivaaseen* – drought, famine, death; break the neck and go to heaven. Incidentally, this dark yet influential poem also accounts for the names of several nearby landmarks: Famine Hill, Neck Heath and Heaven's Hill.

In ancient Finnish culture, death was surrounded by a complex and lyrical paradigm of mythology and ritual. Believers in soul dualism, the Finns subscribed to the idea that a person was inhabited by not one, but three entities: *Henki*, *Luonto* and *Itse*.

The ancient Finns lived in perpetual fear of the dead abandoning their graves and returning to haunt them, either as ghosts or, perhaps more disturbingly, as wild animals. To assuage this fear, and prevent any disagreeable encounters, a succession of elaborate rituals was undertaken at the moment of one's death so that the deceased's soul could find its rightful place in the underworld. To begin with, it was considered bad luck for a person to die without it being witnessed by a member of the living. The corpse was immediately washed, unless the person had committed suicide, in which case the body was left unwashed and buried lying on its stomach in the clothes that they died in. It was considered best, though not imperative, for the dead to be in the ground before sunset. The wooden coffin was nailed shut and a procession carried it by hand to the cemetery, stopping on the way by the home of the deceased so they could 'see' it one final time. In a forest before the cemetery, the funeral procession would make a second stop, and a mark called a *karsikko* was engraved into the trunk of a pine or rowan tree. As with other death rituals, this gesture had metaphysical significance. It formed a kind of invisible border between the world of the living and the land of the dead.

As it was believed that the dead tend to forget they are dead and occasionally try to return home, the *karsikko* marking functioned as a kind of polite reminder to the dead to return to the ground in which they now belonged.

Death, in ancient Finnish society, was the end of one journey but also the beginning of another. It marked the start of a long and solitary voyage across an uncharted landscape, where the temptation to return home, to the land of the living, was forever strong. For the duration of exactly one year following the death of a person, it was forbidden to speak the deceased's name aloud, as it was thought to make them homesick. During this year, the widow was unable to remarry or experience pleasure in the home. On the one-year anniversary of the death, a celebration feast was held in the village as it was believed that the dead had by then successfully found their place in the underworld, a place referred to as Tuonela. Said to exist on the far side of a dark

Lemminkäinen's Mother, Akseli Gallen-Kallela (1897). Lemminkäinen's body was hacked to pieces and thrown into the river of Tuonela. His mother, in a futile attempt to bring him back to life, collected the body parts from the river and stitched him back together.
Finnish National Gallery.

river, Tuonela is a bleak and dismal place where the dead lie in eternal sleep. But even there, the dead are never completely out of reach of the living. Through a shaman, the boundary of death could be transcended. After entering a trance state through a process of dance and ritual, the shaman had to trick the ferryman to take him across the river to Tuonela. Once there, he could commune with the dead, deliver messages or ask for advice and guidance. It was said that if the shaman died during the ritual, he had been captured by the guards of the underworld.

The constructs of modern society act to conceal death and abstract it from life. Ironically, this too is the case in the village of Death. In Persson's photographs, symbols of death border on cliché; a man holding a rifle, corpses of dead foxes in the snow. Gone are the ancient beliefs and rituals that mediated the transition from life to death, the journey from this world to the realm beyond. Death now resides in a different form: the estrangement of a people from its own past; the death of an ancient culture. Yet, this estrangement is not absolute. In the Finnish language, death and melancholy possess their own grammar and vocabulary, one that hints back to ancient Finnish customs and rituals, mythologies and beliefs. It can be found in stories and songs, rhymes and parables; in the names of villages, the films of Kaurismäki and even in Finnish tango. Together, they form a fine thread, one that transcends time and cultures, tenuously binding the world of the living to the land of the dead.

Australia and New Zealand

TRAGEDY POOL
Western Australia

ROAD TO NOWHERE
Tasmania, Australia

MELANCHOLY WATERHOLE
Queensland, Australia

MOUNT HOPELESS
South Australia

**MAMUNGKUKUMPURANGKUNTJUNYA
(WHERE THE DEVIL URINATES)**
South Australia

DISAPPOINTMENT ISLAND
Auckland Islands, New Zealand

MOUNT DISAPPOINTMENT
Victoria, Australia

MURDERING BEACH ROAD
Otago, New Zealand

DISAPPOINTMENT COVE
Southland, New Zealand

NOWHERE ELSE
Tasmania, Australia

USELESS LOOP
Western Australia

SUICIDE BAY
Tasmania, Australia

CAPE GRIM
Tasmania, Australia

DEATH ROAD
New South Wales, Australia

DOUBTFUL ISLAND
Southland, New Zealand

USELESS ISLANDS
Southland, New Zealand

Canada

GLOOMY LAKE
Ontario, Canada

LITTLE HOPE ISLAND
Nova Scotia, Canada

DEATH LAKE
Ontario, Canada

SORROW ISLANDS
British Columbia, Canada

DEAD DOG ISLAND
Ontario, Canada

UNFORTUNATE COVE
Newfoundland, Canada

PAIN LAKE
Ontario, Canada

LAKE TORMENT
Nova Scotia, Canada

REPULSE BAY
Nunavut, Canada

MISTAKE ISLAND
British Columbia, Canada

DEVASTATION ISLAND
British Columbia, Canada

LONELY ISLAND
Ontario, Canada

ROAD TO NOWHERE
Nunavut, Canada

GRUMPY LANE
Nova Scotia, Canada

MURDER ISLAND
Nova Scotia, Canada

UNFORTUNATE COVE
Newfoundland, Canada

KILLER LAKE
Ontario, Canada

MASSACRE ISLAND
Ontario, Canada

NOWHERE ISLAND
Ontario, Canada

SOLITUDE ISLAND
Ontario, Canada

FORLORN LAKE
Ontario, Canada

FUTILE LAKE
Ontario, Canada

POINTLESS MOUNTAIN
British Columbia, Canada

United Kingdom and Ireland

FAIL
UK

PITY ME
Durham, UK

WORLD'S END
Enfield, UK

MELANCHOLY LANE
Wareham, UK

ALL ALONE
Bradford, UK

KILL
Ireland

LABOUR IN VAIN ROAD
Stansted, UK

United States

LITTLE HOPE
Wisconsin, US

DEPRESSION POND
New York, US

GRAVE LAKE
Wyoming, US

BROKEN DREAMS DRIVE
Arizona, US

ROAD TO MISERY
Maine, US

ACCIDENT
Maryland, US

DEAD WOMAN POND
Texas, US

EMPTINESS DRIVE
Texas, US

LOVELESS LAKE
Wisconsin, US

HAUNTED LAKE
New Hampshire, US

ABANDONED
New York, US

FAILURE CANYON
Utah, US

CRYING CHILD ISLAND
Florida, US

DUBIOUS RESERVOIR
Oregon, US

SAD LAKE
Oregon, US

CRYING LADY ROCK
Washington, US

SHADES OF DEATH ROAD
New Jersey, US

MISTAKE ISLAND
Minnesota, US

LAKE OF NO RETURN
Arkansas, US

DESPERATION LAKE
Alaska, US

DEFEATED
Tennessee, U.S

GRIEF ISLAND
Alaska, US

LOST BOYS LANE
Florida, US

MISERABLE LAKE
Illinois, US

LONELYVILLE
New York, US

CALAMITY LAKE
Minnesota, US

SUICIDE BRIDGE
Maryland, US

SUICIDE LAKE
Wyoming, US

DEAD WOMAN'S CROSSING
Oklahoma, US

BLOODY DICK PEAK
Montana, US

BLOODY SPRINGS
Mississippi, US

GRUMPY DOG ROAD
Montana, US

HOPELESS PASS
California, US

HOPELESS WAY
Nevada, US

MOUNT DESPAIR
Montana, US

TERROR LAKE
Alaska, US

DEAD WOMAN POND
Texas, US

BLUNDER POND
Maine, US

STARVATION HEIGHTS
Oregon, US

DEAD WOMAN CREEK
Oklahoma, US

NASTY POND
Oregon, US

NAMELESS
Tennessee, US

MOUNT TERROR
Montana, US

CAPE DISAPPOINTMENT
Washington, US

DOG SLAUGHTER FALLS
Kentucky, US

LONESOME ROAD / LONELY STREET
North Carolina, US

TERMINATION POINT
Washington, US

DESPERATE LANE
North Carolina, US

END OF THE WORLD
California, US

HELL FOR CERTAIN ROAD
Kentucky, US

UNCERTAIN
Texas, US

WHAT CHEER
Iowa, US

BROKEN HEART LANE
Texas, US

DESPERATION DRIVE / SOLITUDE WAY
California, US

PURGATORY POND
New Hampshire, US

LONESOME LAKE
New Hampshire, US

BLUNDER POND
Maine, US

NOTHING
Arizona, US

POINT NO POINT
Washington, US

SAD ROAD
Kentucky, US

POVERTY ISLAND
Michigan, US

MISERY BAY
Michigan, US

DESPAIR ISLAND
Rhode Island, US

CRAZY WOMAN CREEK
Wyoming, US

HEARTACHE ROAD
Montana, US

SLAUGHTER BEACH
Delaware, US

DOOM TOWN
Nevada, US

BUCKET OF BLOOD STREET
Arizona, US

DISAPPOINTMENT LAKE
Idaho, US

WHY ME LORD LANE
South Carolina, US

NIGHTMARE LAKE
Montana, US

MISERABLE ISLAND
Illinois, US

TERRIBLE MOUNTAIN
Vermont, US

BROKEN ISLAND
Washington, US

SPITEFUL GEYSER
Wyoming, US

HATEFUL HILL
Vermont, US

WORTHLESS ROAD
California, US

DISAPPOINTMENT CLEAVER
Washington, US

DISAPPOINTMENT
Washington, US

CAPE DISAPPOINTMENT
Washington, US

DISAPPOINTMENT MOUNTAIN
Minnesota, US

DISAPPOINTMENT ROAD
Kentucky, US

CAMP SUICIDE ROAD
Michigan, US

DISENCHANTMENT BAY
Alaska, US

DEPRESSED LAKE
California, US

Other

DECEPTION ISLAND
Antarctica

SUFFERING STREET
Tunisia

SUFFERING LANE
Bermuda

GRANDMOTHER'S HOLE BEACH
India

ISLA CAJA DE MUERTOS
(COFFIN ISLAND)
Puerto Rico

TUŽNO
(SAD)
Croatia

FEMMINAMORTA
(DEAD WOMAN)
Italy

MISERY
France

PUERTA DEL DIABLO
(PORT OF THE DEVIL)
El Salvador

BAHÍA INÚTIL
(USELESS BAY)
Chile

PURGATÓRIO
(PURGATORY)
Portugal

ANGÚSTIAS
(ANGUISH)
Portugal

CAP MALHEUREUX
(UNFORTUNATE CAPE)
Mauritius

ULTRAMORT
(ULTRA DEATH)
Spain

LARGO DOS AFLITOS
(SQUARE OF THE AFFLICTED)
Brazil

PASKALAMPI
(SHIT LAKE)
Finland

KUOLEMA
(DEATH)
Finland

ALONE
Italy

BOUZILLÉ
(FAILURE)
France

KOTZEN
(VOMITING)
Germany

DIE
France

DIVORCE BEACH
Mexico

HELL
Netherlands

PITY
Haiti

SADNESS STREET
Tunisia

HOPELESS BOULEVARD
Tunisia

PUERTO DEL HAMBRE (PORT FAMINE)
Chile

**ENSAMHETEN
(LONELINESS)**
Sweden

**ESTRADA DAS LÁGRIMAS
(ROAD OF TEARS)**
Brazil

**FINSTERWALDE
(DARK WOODS)**
Germany

**LEIDENSWEG
(SUFFERING WAY)**
Germany

**LEIDENSBERG
(SUFFERING HILL)**
Germany

**DÜSTERSTRASSE
(GLOOMY STREET)**
Germany

**ANGSTWEG
(FEAR WAY)**
Germany

**SORGENWEG
(SORROW WAY)**
Germany

**DÜSTER SEE
(GLOOMY LAKE)**
Germany

**ELEND
(MISERY)**
Germany

**SORGE
(SORROW)**
Germany

AGONY ISLAND
Marshall Islands

UGLY
India

Damien Rudd

Damien Rudd (1984) is an artist and writer, born in Sydney, Australia. He received his MFA from Kunsthøgskolen i Bergen, Norway. He currently lives in Amsterdam, the Netherlands, where he works on a study of Aby Warburg's *Mnemosyne Atlas*. The collection of sad topographies from which this book originated can be found at instagram.com/sadtopographies

Kateryna Didyk

Kateryna Didyk (1990) is an illustrator and printmaker, born in Vinnytsia, Ukraine. She specializes in etching, monotype, watercolour painting and digital art. In 2017, Kateryna graduated from Kyiv National Academy of Fine Art and Architecture where she received her master's degree in printmaking and book illustration. She currently lives and works in Kiev.

katedidyk.com

Acknowledgements

I would like to extend my gratitude to all the people who helped make this book happen. To Kate, for the countless hours she spent hand-drawing the maps. Many thanks to Simon Johnson for his excellent research and editorial input. To Randy Rosenthal for his sharp editorial eye. I extend my gratitude to Justin Falk, Maria Martens, Jay Blair and Tashina Blom for all their time and valuable feedback. I am deeply grateful to my agents Heather Karpas at ICM Partners in New York and Rebecca Ritchie at Curtis Brown in London. To Nicola Crossley and Iain MacGregor at Simon & Schuster. To the various people who read drafts of the book, for their advice I did and did not follow. Lastly to Lieke de Jong for her generous support throughout the writing process.